HIGH SCHOOL BASKETBALL RULES
SIMPLIFIED & ILLUSTRATED
2019-20

DR. KARISSA NIEHOFF, Publisher
Theresia Wynns, Editor
NFHS Publications

To maintain the sound traditions of this sport, encourage sportsmanship and minimize the inherent risk of injury, the National Federation of State High School Associations (NFHS) writes playing rules for varsity competition among student-athletes of high school age. High school coaches, game officials and administrators who have knowledge and experience regarding this particular sport and age group volunteer their time to serve on the rules committee. Member associations of the NFHS independently make decisions regarding compliance with or modification of the playing rules for the student-athletes in their respective states.

NFHS rules are used by education-based and non-education-based organizations serving children of varying skill levels who are of high school age and younger. In order to make NFHS rules skill-level and age-level appropriate, the rules may be modified by any organization that chooses to use them. Except as may be specifically noted in the NFHS Basketball Rules Book, the NFHS makes no recommendation about the nature or extent of the modifications that may be appropriate for children who are younger or less skilled than high school varsity athletes.

Every individual using the NFHS basketball rules is responsible for prudent judgment with respect to each contest, athlete and facility, and each athlete is responsible for exercising caution and good sportsmanship. The NFHS basketball rules should be interpreted and applied so as to make reasonable accommodations for athletes, coaches and officials with disabilities.

2019-20 High School Basketball Rules Simplified & Illustrated

Produced by Referee Enterprises Inc., publishers of *Referee* magazine.

Published by the
NATIONAL FEDERATION
OF STATE HIGH SCHOOL ASSOCIATIONS
PO Box 690
Indianapolis, IN 46206
Phone: 317-972-6900, Fax: 317-822-5700
nfhs.org

ISBN-13: 978-1-58208-438-1

Printed in the United States of America

Table of Contents

Each state high school association adopting the NFHS basketball rules is the sole and exclusive source of binding rules interpretations for contests involving its member schools. Any person having questions about the interpretation of NFHS basketball rules should contact the rules interpreter designated by his or her state high school association.

The NFHS is the sole and exclusive source of model interpretations of NFHS basketball rules. State rules interpreters may contact the NFHS for model basketball rules interpretations. No other model basketball rules interpretations should be considered.

2019-20 NFHS Basketball Rules Changes

Rule Changed	Rule Changed Description
3-4-3e (2)	The option to use the style of the number that uses the team jersey color itself bordered with not less than two ¼-inch solid border(s) contrasting with the team jersey color will be eliminated by 2024-25.
3-5-4b	If worn, only one headband is permitted, it must be worn on the forehead crown. It must be nonabrasive and unadorned, and it must be no more than 3 inches wide.
3-5-4d	The statement "Hair control devices are not required to meet color restrictions" was added to the rule.
3-5-5	NEW NOTE: Provided the shorts are not in conflict with 3-4-5, no drawstring or other part of the shorts intended to maintain them in a normal position causes potential harm to the player or others and wearing of the shorts is not objectionable in exposing the anatomy, there is no restriction on folding or rolling the shorts at the natural waistband seam.

3-5-8	MOUTHGUARD
	1. A tooth and mouth protector (intraoral), if worn must:
	  a. include an occlusal (protecting and separating the biting surfaces) portion;
	  b. include a labial (protecting the teeth and supporting structures) portion;
	  c. cover the posterior teeth with adequate thickness;
	
	2. It is recommended that the protector be properly fitted, protecting the anterior (leading) dental arch and:
	  a. constructed from a model made from an impression of the individual's teeth, or
	  b. constructed and fitted to the individual by impressing the teeth into tooth and mouth protector itself.
	
	3. State associations may deem a tooth and mouth protector required equipment.

10-5-5 NOTE	The head coach and any number of assistant coaches may enter the court in the situation where a fight may break out — or has broken out — to prevent the situation from escalating.

2019-20 Signal Changes

Signal Chart No. 3 .... When a held ball occurs, the covering official(s) must stop the clock using signal No. 2 (straight arm, open palm extended) while simultaneously sounding the whistle, then give the held-ball signal.

2019-20 Major Editorial Changes

9-9-1 Exception .... A ball in team control of Team A in the frontcourt that is deflected by a defensive player, which causes the ball to go into the backcourt, may be recovered by either team unless the offense was the last to touch the ball before it went into the backcourt. If the offense was last to touch the ball in its frontcourt, only the defense can legally recover the basketball.

2019-20 Points of Emphasis

1. Headband and Hair Control Devices

2. Medical Bracelets

3. Throw-in Violations

4. Pre-Game Meeting with Administrator on Crowd Supervision and Control

Part 1

New or Revised Rules

The NFHS Basketball Rules Committee always keeps the following basic objectives before it:

- Fair play so that neither team gains an unfair advantage
- A balance between offense and defense
- Careful definitions of words and expressions
- Keep rules brief and concise
- Avoid exceptions
- Have simple statements
- Properly codify
- Write rules that are proper for level of play
- Minimizing risks to participants
- Use of fundamental statements

These objectives can only be realized as long as the rules are enforced as written and without exception. To set aside a rule which benefits one team or the other diminishes the spirit of fair play.

This simplified and illustrated book is a supplement to the basketball rules book and other materials which are designed to make officiating and coaching easier through uniformity of interpretations and rulings, and standardization of mechanics for game administration.

The rules are based upon sound fundamentals and axioms which make it possible for those studying them to apply certain basic principles rather than resorting to rote memory in the study and teaching of rules. Hundreds of administrators, coaches and officials have contributed to the logical development of the NFHS basketball rules.

The NFHS Basketball Rules Committee annually considers many items which were submitted as potential changes or revisions. The items which secured favorable endorsement are listed on page 6 of this book. The majority of illustrations in Part I show these additions and revisions. These illustrations are intended to answer the obvious questions which are raised in regard to the new rules.

When possible, some illustrations are presented to cover the "Points of Emphasis" identified by the committee. In some cases, a future rule change may have to be enacted in response to this problem area.

The illustrations found in Part II of this book have been edited to reflect any changes or clarifications as directed by the committee. Recent interpretations have been added to keep the contents current.

NOTE: Unless specifically indicated, all illustrations involve a two-point try and not a three-point try. When applicable, Team A always refers to the team in possession of the ball. Team B refers to the defensive team.

3-4-3e(2) Effective 2024-25, the option to have jersey numbers the same color as the predominant color of the jersey will be eliminated.

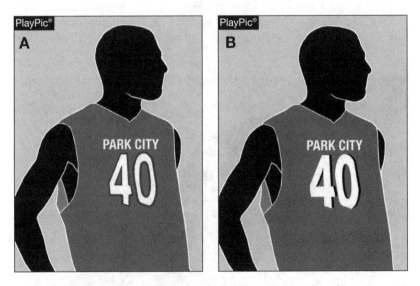

3-4-3e(1 & 3) Two legal jersey numbering options still remain:
- a solid contrasting number with no more than two solid color ¼-inch borders around the entire number (PlayPic A).
- a solid contrasting color with a "shadow" trim of a contrasting color on part of the number not to exceed ½ inch in width and may be used with one ¼-inch border (PlayPic B).

3-5-4b A headband is any item that goes around the entire head. It must be a circular design without extensions. If worn, only one is permitted, it must be worn on the forehead/crown, it must be nonabrasive and unadorned, and shall be no more than 3 inches wide. The headband has color restrictions that must be followed.

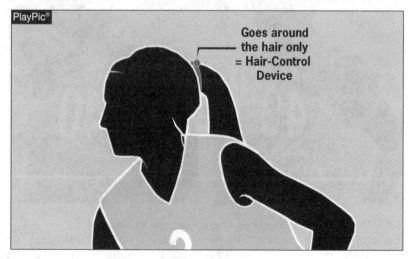

Goes around
the hair only
= Hair-Control
Device

3-5-4d A hair-control device is not required to meet color restrictions. Hair control devices only go around hair, not the entire head.

3-5-5 There are no restrictions on rolling shorts at the natural waistband seam, so long as
- they do conflict with rule 3-4-5;
- multiple manufacturers logos are not visible;
- the drawstring does not present a safety hazard;
- the anatomy is sufficiently covered.

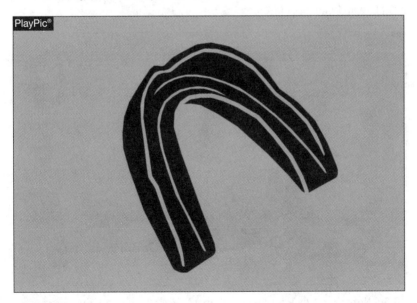

3-5-8 New Mouthguards are legal, so long as they meet provisions regarding their components and are properly fitted. State associations may deem them required equipment.

10-5-5 Note Assistant coaches are now allowed to come onto the playing floor to help break up a fight.

10-5-5 Note Stop Clock for Held Ball: In a held-ball situation, the covering official should first blow the whistle while simultaneously using the stop clock signal (signal 2), and then progress to the held ball signal (signal 3).

9-9-1 Exception Updates language to read: "A ball in team control of Team A in the frontcourt that is deflected by a defensive player, which causes the ball to go into the backcourt, may be recovered by either team unless the offense was the last to touch the ball before it went into the backcourt. If the offense was last to touch the ball it its frontcourt, only the defense can legally recover the basketball."

Part 2
New or Revised POEs

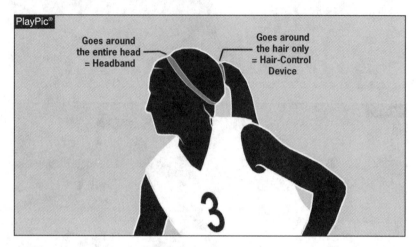

Goes around
the entire head
= Headband

Goes around
the hair only
= Hair-Control
Device

3

POE: Hair control devices and headbands
• Headbands go around the entire head and have color restrictions.
• Hair control devices only go around hair, and do not have color restrictions.

5

POE: Silicone/metal Bracelets
Silicone bracelets that provide medical information, like their metal counterparts, may be worn so long as the bracelet is taped down to the wrist with the medical information showing.

POE: Pregame meeting with administrators/crowd control: Game officials should meet with a school administrator prior to their pregame to discuss supervision and crowd control. Officials should not be responsible for crowd control.

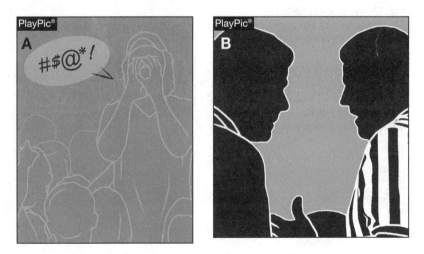

POE: Pregame meeting with administrators/crowd control
Should a fan need to be removed during the contest (PlayPic A), game officials should notify school administrators and allow school administrators to handle the problem (PlayPic B).

POE: Throw-in Violations

The throw-in and the throw-in count **begin** when the ball is at the disposal of a player of the team entitled to it.

The throw-in **ends** when:

a. The passed ball touches or is touched by another player in-bounds.

b. The passed ball touches or is touched by another player out-of-bounds. except as in 7-5-7.

c. The throw-in team commits a violation.

POE: Throw-in Violations

The designated throw-in spot is 3 feet wide with no depth limitation and is established and signaled by the official prior to putting the ball at the thrower's disposal. Pivot foot restrictions are not in affect for a designated throw-in. The thrower must keep one foot on or over the designated spot until the ball is released.

Violation - To leave the designated throw-in spot prior to releasing the ball.

POE: Throw-in Violations

Violation - To pass the ball so it goes directly out of bounds prior to touching another player.

POE: Throw-in Violations

Violation - To pass the ball so it is touched by a a teammate while on the out-of-bounds side of the throw-in boundary-line plane, except in 7-5-7.

POE: Throw-in Violations

Violation - To not release the ball on a pass directly into the court before five seconds have elapsed.

Part 3
Rule 1

Court and Diagram

The playing court shall be a rectangular surface free from obstructions and with dimensions not greater than 94 feet in length by 50 feet in width. Ideal measurements for high school competition are 84 feet by 50 feet. There shall be at least 3 feet (preferably 10 feet) of unobstructed space outside the boundaries.

The backboards shall be of any rigid material and either transparent or nontransparent. The front surface shall be flat and, unless it is transparent, it shall be white. Tinted glass backboards are prohibited beginning with those manufactured after January 1, 1995. The backboard shall either be fan-shaped or rectangular, with specifications as found in the rules book. The bottom and each side of a rectangular backboard shall be padded according to specifications. The backboards shall be the same size at both ends of the court. No logo, marking or lettering is permitted on any part of the backboard, backboard padding, or basket. The padding shall be a single solid color and be the same color on both backboards.

Each basket shall consist of a single metal ring, 18 inches in inside diameter. Each ring shall be securely attached to the backboard. Either nonmovable or movable rings are legal. The upper edge of the basket ring shall be 10 feet above and parallel to the floor.

The rules book also contains detailed specifications on the required backboard padding as well as specifications for moveable basket rings. Also listed is an organization to contact for information regarding court lighting specifications.

SHADOW LINE IS 1/4 INCH WIDE

CENTER RESTRAINING CIRCLE AND DIVISION LINE MAINTAIN A 2 INCH WIDTH

1-3-1 The center restraining circle can have a minimum of a 1/4-inch wide single line but a line no wider than 2 inches to designate the outer edge of the circle. Many existing courts already have a center circle that has a 1/4-inch line. Contrasting colored-floor areas are still permissible.

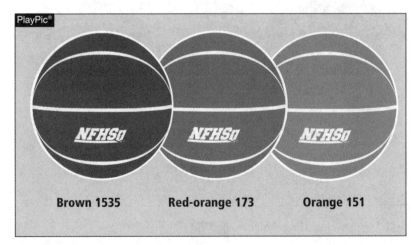

Brown 1535   **Red-orange 173**   **Orange 151**

1-12a The rule specifies the ball color using Pantone Matching System numbers for the three colors allowed, effective 2019-2020.

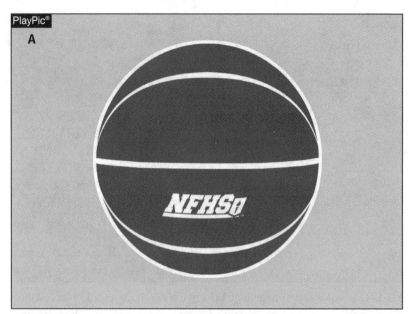

1-12-1c A legal game ball, as shown in PlayPic A, shall have a deeply-pebbled, granulated surface with horizontally shaped panels bonded tightly to the rubber carcass.

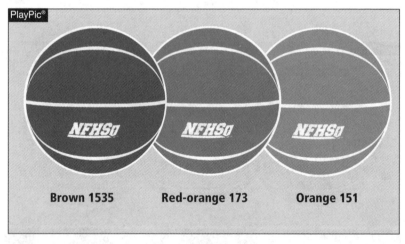

Brown 1535   **Red-orange 173**   **Orange 151**

1-12-1c Reminder: The pebbled, granulated surface is in conjunction with the inclusion of the NFHS Authenticating Mark and featuring one of three approved colors, effective 2019-20.

APPROVED ORANGE OR NATURAL TAN COLOR
BLACK RUBBER RIB NO WIDER THAN 1/4 INCH

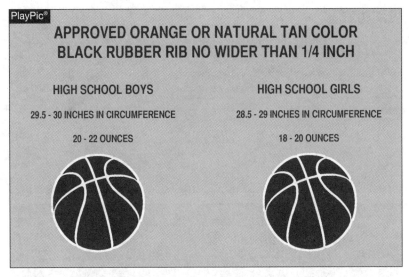

HIGH SCHOOL BOYS	HIGH SCHOOL GIRLS
29.5 - 30 INCHES IN CIRCUMFERENCE	28.5 - 29 INCHES IN CIRCUMFERENCE
20 - 22 OUNCES	18 - 20 OUNCES

1-12-1d; 1-12-3 The referee is the sole judge as to the ball's legality. The home team shall provide a ball which meets the specifications. If the home team is unable to do so, the referee may select one furnished by the visiting team. By state association adoption either a boy's or girl's size legal ball may be used for junior high school boys' competition.

1-12-1g The ball shall include the NFHS Authenticating Mark. The mark can be displayed in either format shown. A current list of NFHS authenticated products can be found on the Web site, nfhs.org. If an official discovers that the playing ball does not carry the NFHS authenticating mark, the contest is still to be played provided there is at least one otherwise legal ball that can be used. The official shall inform the coach that a report will be sent to the state association for their review.

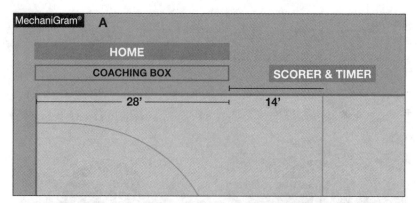

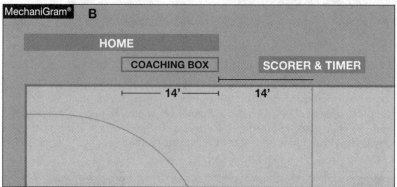

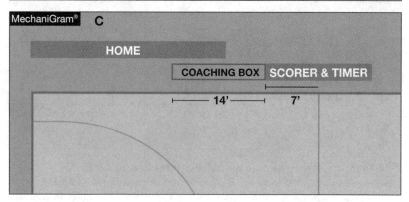

1-13-2 State associations have the ability to alter the location and length of the coaching box. The maximum length of the coaching box cannot exceed 28 feet. In MechaniGram A, the traditional endline to 28-foot mark coaching box is used and legal. In MechaniGram B, the 14-foot coaching box is placed from 28-foot mark and back toward the endline (as done in recent years) and is legal. In MechaniGram C, the 14-foot coaching box is relocated to be centered around the 28-foot mark and would be illegal (the 28-foot mark is furthest to the table).

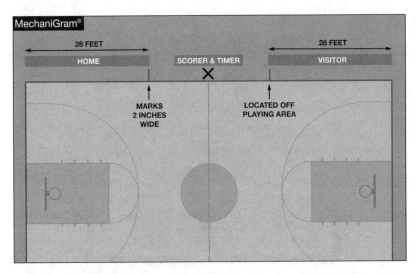

1-13-2; 1-17; 10-6-1 By state association adoption, an optional coaching box may be authorized. If used, the optional coaching box may be a maximum of 28 feet. State associations may alter the length and placement of the 28-foot coaching box. An "X" is required on the floor in front of the official scorer.

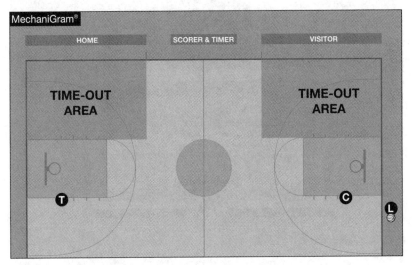

1-13-3; 5-11-2; 5-11-3 The time-out area shall be the area inside an imaginary rectangle formed by the boundaries of the sideline (including the bench), end line and imaginary line extended from the free-throw lane line nearest the bench meeting and imaginary line extended from the coaching box line.

1-14; 5-6-2 When a red light behind the backboard (1) or an LED light on the backboard (2) is present, it is permitted to signal the expiration of time in the quarter/extra period. If no red/LED light is present, the audible timer's signal will signal the expiration of time.

1-19 1) The use of electronic devices are permitted during the game.
2) Use of a tablet courtside for coaching purposes is permitted.

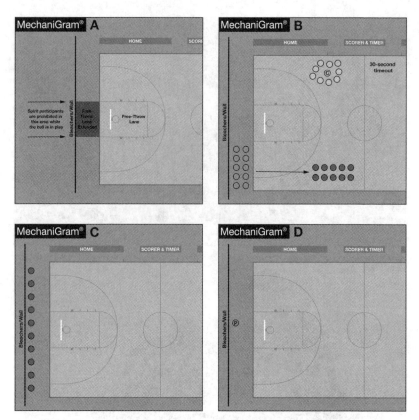

1-20 In MechaniGram A, the prohibited area is displayed in gray. In MechaniGram B, illegal as non-playing personnel shall remain outside of the playing area during a 30-second or less time-out during the game. In MechaniGram C and D, illegal as non-playing personnel shall stand outside the free-throw lane lines extended toward the sidelines throughout the game.

Part 3
Rule 2

Officials and Their Duties

The game officials are an important and necessary part of each basketball game. Officials must accept the responsibility of enforcing the letter as well as the spirit of the rules. Basketball officiating is not an easy task. The basketball official must be alert, quick and physically fit in order to be in the proper position to monitor the action of 10 players over the entire court. The game is demanding but it is also rewarding because the officials are vital to the game.

Good officiating is partially dependent on a thorough knowledge of the rules and the related material and use of the proper mechanics and approved signals. Most decisions on the court must be made so quickly that they must come by reflex. The only way the proper reflexes can be developed is through continual study and practice. Basic fundamentals then become second nature, and correct decisions are virtually automatic. The individual who officiates in games played under the NFHS rules is extremely fortunate for there is an abundance of study material available. The high schools and their state associations provide training and proving grounds for many officials. A crew of either two or three officials may be used.

When an official accepts a game assignment, his or her responsibility is clear and well defined. The officials must make certain the game is played within the rules so that each team has an opportunity to exhibit its best. The responsibility for teaching the rules is that of the coach who must design offensive and defensive strategies which are within the rules.

2-1-3 It is recommended that the official scorer and timer be seated next to each other. It improves game administration when this is done. However, in some facilities it may not be possible.

2-2-1 Note A state association may permit game or replay officials to use a replay monitor during state championship series contests to determine if a try for goal at the expiration of time in the fourth quarter or any overtime period (0:00 on the game clock) should be counted, and if so, determine if it is a two- or a three-point goal.

**GAME TIME
8:00 P.M.**

2-2-2; 2-2-4 The officials shall arrive on the floor at least 15 minutes prior to the scheduled starting time of the game. The officials' jurisdiction extends from their arrival on the floor until the referee approves the final score. When all officials leave the visual confines of the playing area at the end of the game, jurisdiction has ended and the score has been approved. Each official has specific pregame duties and responsibilities to take care of before the game begins. The use of either two or three officials is authorized.

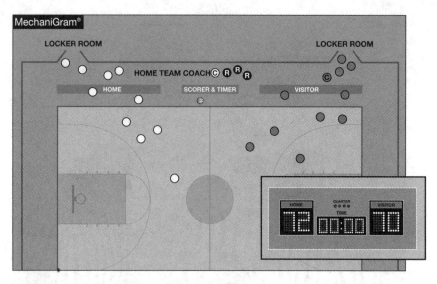

2-2-4 The Team A coach confronts the referee immediately following the game. Even though the officials had left the playing court, all officials had not left the visual confines of the playing area. The technical foul free throws will be attempted and if both are successful, an extra period will be played.

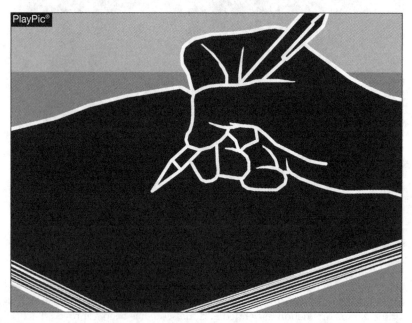

2-2-4 A note was added clarifying the administrative responsibilities of game officials through the completion of required reports.

2-8-5; 3-3-8 Any player who exhibits signs, symptoms or behaviors consistent with a concussion, such as loss of consciousness, headache, dizziness, confusion or balance problems, shall be immediately removed from play and shall not return until cleared by an appropriate health-care professional. If No. 32 appears at the scorer's table to reenter the game, the officials shall assume the coach/school followed the appropriate return-to-play procedures and No. 32 is eligible to participate.

2-9-1 Officials should report fouls to the scorer by using two hands to displays the fouler's number. The official's right hand will indicate the first digit (tens or "two" in the PlayPic example) and the left hand will show a second digit (ones or "four"), so it appears in a left-to-right sequence to the scorer. When reporting, the official should verbalize 24, not two-four.

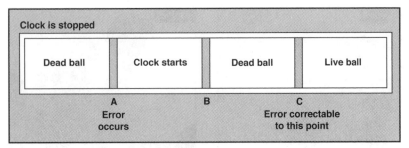

Clock is stopped			
Dead ball	Clock starts	Dead ball	Live ball

A Error occurs	**B**	**C** Error correctable to this point

2-10-2 When an error occurs with the ball dead and the clock stopped (point A), applying the sequence above will help in determining if the error is still correctable.

PlayPic®

2-11-12 The official scorer is now required to wear a black-and-white vertically striped garment.

2-12-4; 5-11-2 The timer shall sound a warning signal 15 seconds before the expiration of an intermission or 60-second charged time-out and at 15 seconds of a 30-second time-out.

2-12-5; 10-6-2 The interval of time to replace a disqualified or injured player, or a player directed to leave the game, is 15 seconds. A warning horn will be sounded immediately upon the notification from the official to begin the interval.

2-12-5 Note A note was added to clarify when the 15-second interval of time begins to replace an injured play. Once the player is injured in (1), the player is removed from the court (2). At that point, the coach should be informed that a replacement is required (3) before signaling the timer to begin the 15-second interval of time (4). The coach can choose at that point to use a time-out to keep the injured player in the game, but the player must be ready to play by the conclusion of the time-out.

Part 3
Rule 3

Players, Substitutes and Equipment

The substitution rule in basketball is extremely liberal. A substitute may replace a player any time the ball is dead and the clock is stopped. After a player has been replaced, such player may not return to the game until the next substitution opportunity after the clock has been properly started following his or her replacement.

A substitute who desires to enter shall report to the scorers, giving his or her number. Substitutions between halves shall be made to the official scorer by the substitute(s) or a team representative prior to the warning signal which sounds 15 seconds before the intermission ends.

At least 10 minutes before the scheduled game starting time, each team must supply the scorers with the name and number of each team member who may participate and also designate starters. After this time period has been reached, a technical foul is charged for not complying with either or both requirements. It also is a maximum one technical foul per team after this time period has been reached, for adding a name(s) to the team member list, changing a team member or player's number, having a player change to the number in the book, or a change in the starting lineup unless the change in starting lineup is necessitated by illness or injury or to attempt a technical-foul free throw.

Player uniforms must conform to listed specifications. These regulations have been adopted to assure ease of identification and to eliminate confusion for scorers, officials, players, coaches and spectators. If there is a question concerning legality of any equipment, the referee shall make the final decision.

3-2; 10-1-1 The name and number of each team member who may participate plus the names of the designated five starting players for each team shall be given to the scorer at least 10 minutes prior to the scheduled starting time of the game. After the time limit has been reached, a team is charged with one technical foul for failure to comply with either or both requirements. It is recommended the team members' numbers be entered into the scorebook in numerical order.

3-2-2; 10-1-2 The scorer beckons the official and reports that all players of one team have different numbers on their shirts than those listed in the scorebook. The offending team is charged with one technical foul even though five infractions occurred. Either the numbers must be changed in the scorebook or the shirts must be changed to match the scorebook numbers. The two technical-foul free throws are administered to begin play.

3-2-2; 10-1-2 A substitute reports to enter but is wearing a number different than that listed for him in the scorebook. The coach informs the scorer that the substitute will not enter, thus avoiding the technical foul and penalty. Since no change had to be made by the scorer, no penalty is assessed.

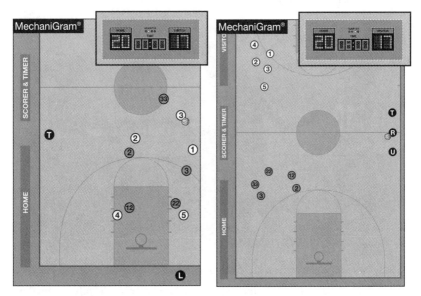

3-3-1a Note; 4-34-2 Clarified that when a substitute is not properly reported, the players in the game at the conclusion of the quarter/when the time-out was granted shall begin play for the new quarter/after the time-out.

3-3-1c Exception If any player has been directed to leave the game, an exception permits substitutes who have legally reported to the scorer to enter the game before the last free throw. By rule, players can be directed to leave the game due to disqualification, injury, bleeding, or an illegal uniform. All substitutes meeting this exception may enter the game until the official has beckoned the required sub onto the floor. At that time, any additional substitutes reporting to the table must wait until after the first of two or the second of three free throws to enter the game.

3-3-3; 4-34 A substitute becomes a player when he or she legally enters the court. If entry is not legal, the substitute becomes a player when the ball becomes live. A player becomes bench personnel after his or her substitute becomes a player or after notification of the coach following his or her disqualification.

3-3-3 Number 4 runs onto the court without being beckoned by an official, while the ball is live. The penalty for this infraction is a technical foul. If the official fails to detect the illegal entry and it is detected by the scorer, he or she may call it to the official's attention. When this error occurs and it is not immediately penalized, it may be corrected, provided it is recognized before the ball becomes live following the first dead ball after the infraction occurred.

3-3-4, 3-3-6 The official stops play for an apparently injured player. Number 35 is actually not hurt and wishes to remain in the game. Since the official has not beckoned for assistance and no bench personnel have entered the court, the player may stay in the game and play is resumed immediately following the few seconds of delay.

3-3-5, 3-5-4 Uniforms shall be worn properly. Shirt tails shall be tucked in. PlayPics 1 and 2 show illegal examples; pants will be worn as manufactured. However, jerseys manufactured to be worn outside the pants are legal as in (3).

3-3-5 During playing action, No. 21's shirt comes out of his pants. However, as play continues, he does not tuck the shirt in even though he has had an opportunity to do so. In (3), the official halts play during the first dead-ball period and directs No. 21 to leave the game.

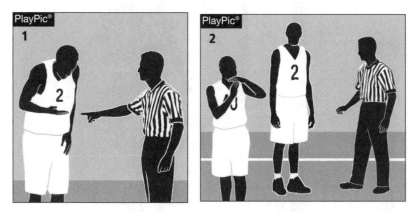

3-3-6, 3-3-7 In (1), play is halted because of the bleeding finger. In (2), a time-out is requested by No. 10. If No. 2 is ready to play at the end of the time-out, he may remain in the game. This also applies to a player with any amount of blood on the jersey; provided the situation is corrected.

Darker of School's Color Scheme (Recommended)

3-4-1c Note It is recommended that the visiting team's dark jersey be the darker of the school's color scheme or black.

3-4-1c The home team shall wear white jerseys and the visiting team dark jerseys.

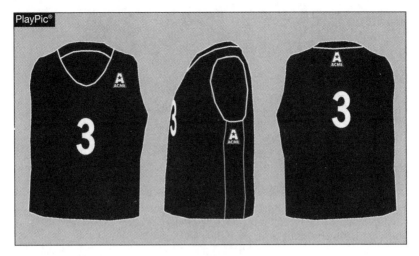

3-4-2a A visible manufacturer's logo/trademark reference is permitted on the team jersey. It may be located no more than five inches below the shoulder seam on the front of the jersey, or two inches from the neckline on the back of the jersey; or in either side insert.

3-4-2b By state association adoption, one commemorative/memorial patch, not to exceed four-square inches, may be worn on the jersey. The patch shall not be a number and must be located above the neckline or in the side insert.

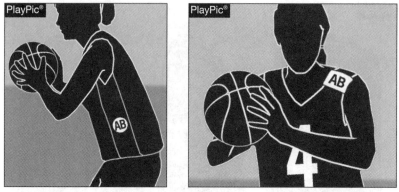

3-4-2c Permits a commemorative/memorial patch, not exceeding four-square inches, to be worn on the jersey provided it is not a number and it is worn above the neckline or in the side insert.

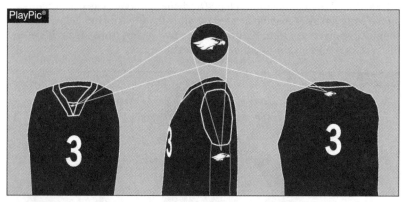

3-4-2d A school or conference logo/mascot may be located at the apex/opening of the neckline, in the corresponding area on the back of the jersey and/or in either side insert.

3-4-4a If used, lettering is permitted in the form of a school's name, a school's nickname, a player's name or an abbreviation of the school's official name. PlayPics A, B and C are all legal examples.

PlayPic®

Legal	Illegal

THE HOPE
1 inch
12
1 inch
SCHOOL

SOUTHPORT HIGH SCHOOL
12
1 inch
CARDINALS

3-4-4 Team names and/or abbreviations may include initials. Horizontal lettering may be arched, but the first and last letters must be on the same horizontal plane, and the plane shall not be below a plane extending through the top of the number(s). Arched lettering below a number must have the first and last letters on the same horizontal plane and the plane shall not be above a plane extending through the bottom of the numbers(s). Any point on any letter shall not be closer than one inch to any point on any number(s).

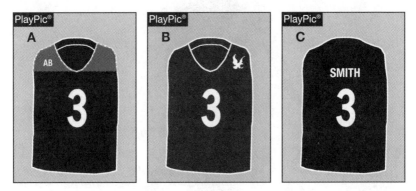

PlayPic®

A
AB
3

B
3

C
SMITH
3

3-4-4b In PlayPic A, the shoulder area is identified and a similar area in the back is a legal area for the allowable identifying names; however, the initials of a player are shown which is an illegal example. In PlayPic B, a school logo would be allowed. In PlayPic C, the last name of a player is shown which is an legal.

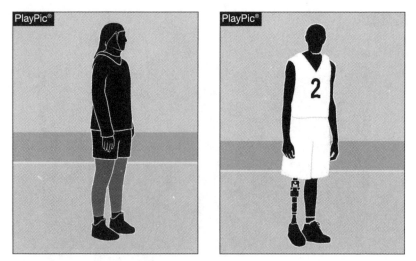

3-5-1 Note Accommodations to participants with disabilities and/or special needs, made by state associations, should not fundamentally alter the sport, heighten risk to the athlete/others or place opponents at a disadvantage.

3-5-1, 4-34-4 The referee shall not permit any team member to wear equipment or apparel which, in his or her judgment, is dangerous or confusing to other players or is not appropriate. This includes the pre-game warm-up period.

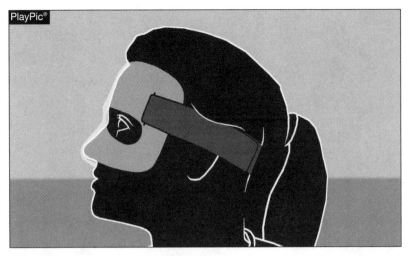

3-5-2 Guards, casts and braces must meet specific guidelines. A protective facemask shall be worn molded to the face.

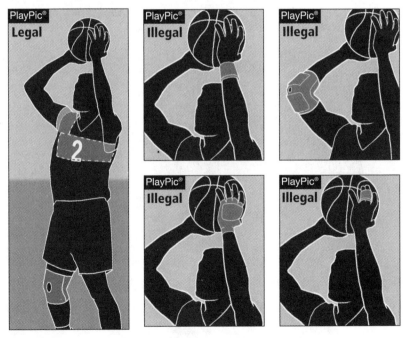

3-5-2a, b A brace, guard or cast made of leather, plaster, pliable (soft) plastic, metal or any hard surface — even though covered with cloth or padding — may NOT be worn on the finger, hand, wrist or elbow. If properly padded, hard substances may be worn on the upper arm or shoulder.

3-5-3 Arm, knee and lower-leg sleeves, compression shorts, and tights, are permissible without a medical reason.

ILLEGAL   **LEGAL**

3-5-3, 3-5-4 All players of the team must have the same color sleeves/tights, compression shorts, headbands and wristbands if worn.

3-5-6 Undershirts shall be a single solid color similar to the torso of the jersey and shall be hemmed and not have frayed or ragged edges. If the undershirt has sleeves, they shall be the same length. See 3-6 for logo requirements. Legal in PlayPic A and B. Illegal in PlayPic C. Only one visible logo is permitted as in 3-6.

3-5-3, 3-5-3b, 3-5-3c and 3-6 Arm sleeves, knee sleeves, lower-leg sleeves, tights and compression shorts are permissible. The sleeves/tights and compression shorts shall be black, white, beige or the predominant color of the jersey and the color sleeves/ tights worn by teammates. All sleeves/ tights and compression shorts shall be the same solid color and must be the same color as any headband or wristband worn.

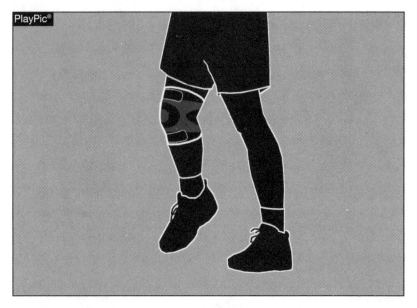

3-5-3 Note A brace is defined as anything worn for a medical purpose to increase stability. In general, it is made of the neoprene or elastic knit with an insert embedded to support the joint. It may or may not have a hinge and/or straps or an opening over the knee cap.

3-5-4 Headbands and sweatbands must be the same color for all team members. Number 55 would be forced to remove the gray wristband to conform to the colors of the other team members.

3-5-4a The rule states that headbands and wristbands shall be white, black, beige or predominant color of the uniform, provided all team members are wearing the same color for each item for all participants. Team members are permitted to wear headbands and wristbands that are white, black, beige or the predominant color of the jersey.

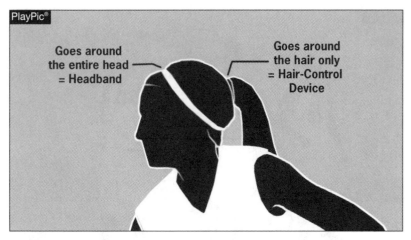

Goes around the entire head = Headband

Goes around the hair only = Hair-Control Device

3-5-4b A headband is defined as any item that goes around the entire head. A hair-control device goes around the hair only and is not subjected to any color requirements.

3-5-4c In (1), the wristband is legal as it is worn below the elbow is less than four inches in length. In (2), the wristband needs to be removed or adjusted to below the elbow before the player can participate.

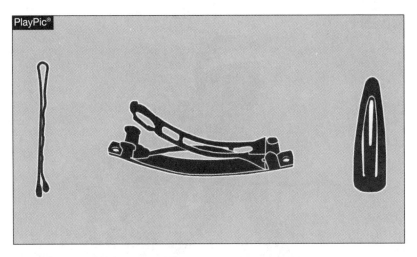

3-5-4d Hard items worn on the head, such as beads, barrettes and bobby pins, are prohibited.

3-5-6 Two of the players are not wearing undershirts while three are wearing them. Even though the length of undershirt sleeves vary from player to player, they are legal as each individual player's undershirt sleeves are the same length on both arms.

3-6-1, 3-4-2a, 3-4-5 One visible manufacturer's logo/trademark/reference or school logo/mascot is permitted on each of the items of player apparel as shown. The logo/trademark/reference may not exceed 2 1/4 square inches and not exceeding 2 1/4 inches in any dimension. There is no restriction on size of logo/trademark/reference for warm-up apparel, including shooting shirts. Because these items of apparel are not worn by players in the game, the logo/trademark/reference restrictions do not apply. A visible manufacturer's logo/trademark/reference is permitted on the team jersey. It may be located no more than five inches below the shoulder seam on the front of the jersey, or two inches from the neckline on the back of the jersey; or in either side insert.

Part 3
Rule 4

Definitions

Coaches and officials have a tendency to overlook Rule 4, thinking that definitions are not as important as, for example, those situations dealing with various types of rules infractions and their respective penalties. Rule 4 is the most important rule in the book.

Basketball definitions apply specifically to basketball rules. A wealth of information is crowded into each definition. Some examples are:

1. **Alternating possession** is a method of putting the ball in play by a throw-in for all jump-ball situations other than the start of the game and each extra period.

2. **Bench personnel** are all individuals who are part of or affiliated with a team, including substitutes, head coach, assistant coach(s), manager(s), statistician(s), etc.

3. **A bonus free throw** is the second free throw awarded for a common foul, except player-control or team-control fouls.

4. **A double personal foul** is a situation in which two opponents commit personal fouls against each other at approximately the same time.

5. **Dunking or stuffing** is the driving, forcing, pushing or attempting to force a ball through the basket with the hand(s).

6. **Kicking the ball** is intentionally striking it with any part of the leg or foot.

7. **A pass** is movement of the ball caused by a player who throws, bats or rolls the ball to another player.

8. **Resumption-of-play procedure** is used to prevent delay in putting the ball in play when a throw-in team does not make a thrower available or following a time-out or intermission (unless either team is not on the court to start the second half). The procedure results in a violation instead of a technical foul for initial delay in specific situations.

9. **A rule** is one of a group of regulations which governs the game.

10. **A try** for field goal is an attempt by a player to score two or three points by throwing the ball into a team's own basket.

4-1 Airborne shooter No. 32 has been fouled in the act of shooting. The defender moved into No. 32's landing spot after he was airborne. Two free throws will be awarded as the try was unsuccessful. The act of shooting includes the airborne shooter.

PlayPic® 1

PlayPic® 2

◄POSS

4-3-3 A dunk during warm-ups is a technical foul and results in two free throws for the opponents plus the ball for a division line throw-in opposite the table. The alternating-possession arrow is set immediately when the ball is at the disposal of thrower No. 4 in (2) as team control is gained at that point for purposes of the alternating-possession arrow. The arrow is then immediately set pointing in the direction of B's basket. Team B will have the first opportunity to make an alternating-possession throw-in.

4-4-6 When the dribbler is unable to advance to frontcourt because of defensive pressure at one point, she may go into the backcourt and cross somewhere else. The 10-second count continues until the ball and both feet of the dribbler are touching entirely in the frontcourt as the ball then has frontcourt location.

4-4-7d The ball is at the disposal of a player when it is available after a goal and the official begins the throw-in count.

4-5-2 Number 4 is confused and dunks the ball in B's basket. The covering official stops play after the dunk and credits the two points to Team B. Team A will then be given the ball for a throw-in from anywhere outside the end line.

4-5-4 Both teams have gone the wrong direction to start the game. Even though considerable time has elapsed and points have been scored at each basket, nothing will be erased. The points will be scored as if the teams had gone the right direction. All fouls, violations, time consumed, etc., will stand and the game will resume from the point of interruption with both teams being instructed to go the right way. This procedure is used regardless of when it occurs.

4-11, 6-7-7 Exception C A continuous-motion foul can only occur when there is a personal or technical foul by the defense on a try. Continuous motion begins with the start of a try in (1) and ends when the ball is clearly in flight in (2). In a free-throw situation, a delayed ruling by the official would result when there is a foul by an opponent of the free thrower.

4-12-1, 6-4-7 If a jumper catches the tossed ball before it touches the floor or a non-jumper, a violation has occurred. The opponents will be awarded a throw-in and the arrow will be set toward the offending team.

4-12 This is an example of team control. It is team control during a pass between teammates. In situations involving deflected passes, fumbles, an interrupted dribble, etc., team control continues until the opponents gain control or the ball becomes dead. There is no team control during a jump ball, or when the ball is in flight during a try or tap for goal.

4-12-1; 4-12-2; 4-12-6 Team control exists during a throw-in when the thrower-in has the ball at his/her disposal. The change primarily affects how foul penalties will be administered. Should there be a foul by a player from the team throwing the ball in, the opposing team would get the ball for a throw-in.

4-15-3 Legal method of starting a dribble. The ball leaves the hand before the pivot foot is lifted. The dribble may be started by pushing, throwing or batting the ball to the floor. A dribble is ball movement caused by a player in control.

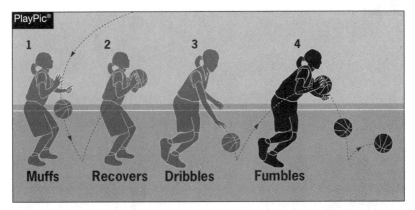

4-15-4 The player muffs the pass, but she recovers and then starts a legal dribble. When she fumbles as in (4), she may recover the ball but may not start a new dribble as the dribble has ended. The term fumble denotes the ball unintentionally slipping from the player's grasp. The ball must be caught with one or both hands before it can be fumbled.

4-15-4b In (1) the dribbler palms/carries the ball by allowing it to come to rest in the hand, thus ending the dribbling. The violation occurs in (2) when a second dribble is started. The proper signal is given to indicate the violation following the stop-clock signal for a violation.

4-15-4d; 9-5-2 A dribble ends when the loss of control by the dribbler is caused by the opponent touching, or being touched by, the ball rather than an intentional batting of the ball.

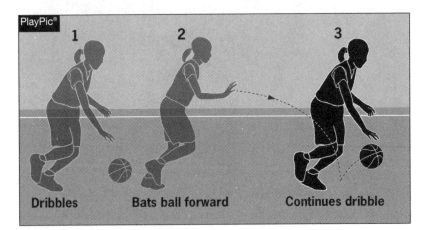

1 Dribbles **2** Bats ball forward **3** Continues dribble

4-15-5 During the dribble, the player bats the ball forward. She can continue the dribble as it has not ended. The distance the ball is batted has no significance.

4-18-2 Number 21 dunks over his opponent and then verbally taunts him. The opponent retaliates and begins fighting. In this situation both players are disqualified for fighting. When the unsporting action of one player causes an opponent to fight, both are charged with fighting.

4-19-3 Number 41 is fouled on a drive to the basket in (1). The contact is ruled to be excessive and an intentional personal foul is correctly charged in (2).

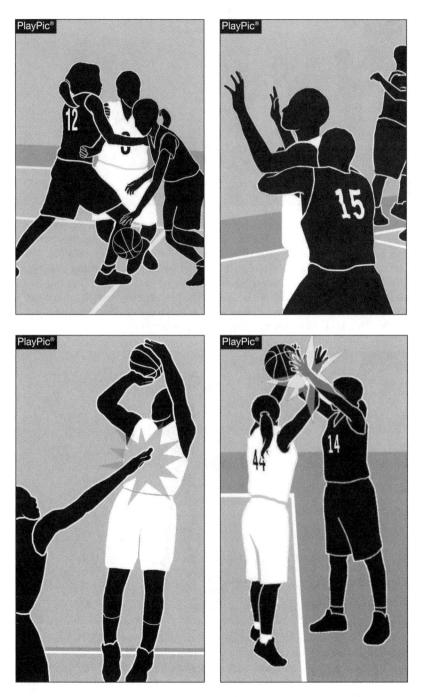

4-19-3d Excessive contact committed by any player is an intentional foul.

4-19-6 Number 5 has control of the ball, and he is on the floor. Number 3 moves to get in position at the last moment; but he is stationary, has both feet on the court, is facing his opponent and is not moving toward No. 5 at the time contact occurs. Since No. 3 has obtained a legal guarding position, this is a player-control foul on No. 5. The official must be sure that the defensive player does not move toward the player with the ball and cause the contact as the defensive player is often moving from the side at an angle. Position is most important on this type of play.

4-19-6 Number 3 has legal position on the court before No. 32 becomes airborne. The foul is on No. 32, the goal does not count if it is made because it is a player-control foul. A player-control foul causes the ball to become dead immediately. Number 32 is an airborne shooter after releasing the ball on a try until he returns to the floor.

4-19-6 This is a player-control foul. Number 5 obtained legal guarding position in the dribbler's path and maintained legal position. The guard is not required to have either or both feet on the court at contact after the initial legal position has been obtained. It would be impossible to move to maintain a legal position if it were required. If the dribbler gets head and shoulders past the guard's torso, contact thereafter is a blocking foul.

4-19-6 Number 4 is an airborne shooter when he fouls the defender in (2). This is a player-control foul. There can be no score whether or not the ball goes through the basket or whether the foul occurs before or after the ball goes through the basket. The player-control foul causes the ball to become dead immediately. No free throw(s) for No. 3. A throw-in for Team B at the nearest out-of-bounds spot follows.

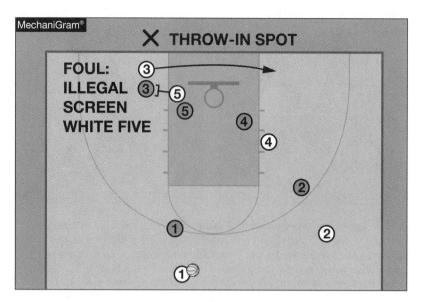

MechaniGram®

✕ THROW-IN SPOT

FOUL:
ILLEGAL
SCREEN
WHITE FIVE

4-19-7; 7-5-5 A5 sets an illegal screen on B3. This is a team-control foul. Team B will be awarded a throw-in at a designated spot nearest to where the foul occurred, even if in the bonus.

PlayPic®

4-19-8a No free throws are awarded for a double personal foul, even though one or both fouls may be flagrant or intentional. Number 2 and No. 15 are disqualified from the game for fighting. The ball will be put in play at the point of interruption.

4-19-8b The four players who are fighting constitute two flagrant double technical fouls. All four players are disqualified. When a double technical foul occurs, no free throws will be awarded and play resumes at the point of interruption.

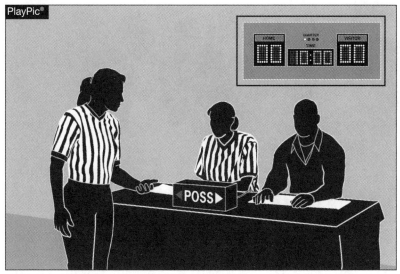

4-19-10 Ten minutes before the game is scheduled to begin, the scorer informs the referee that neither team has submitted a roster or designated starters. This is a simultaneous technical foul by opponents. No free throws will be awarded. The game will begin with a jump ball, as this is the point of interruption.

4-23 Number 2 is running toward his basket but is looking back to receive an outlet pass. Number 3 has obtained a position in No. 2's path with both feet on the floor and facing the opponent. When No. 2 catches the ball and then runs into No. 3, it is a player-control foul. Once No. 2 has the ball, any contact with an opponent who is in legal position is No. 2's responsibility.

4-23-5 Number 3 has obtained a legal position. In obtaining a legal guarding position on a player without the ball, the guard must have both feet on the floor and must be facing the opponent. Time and distance must be sufficient to permit No. 4 to stop or change direction. The distance allowable is determined by the speed of No. 4. The distance never has to exceed two steps, regardless of how fast the opponent is moving.

4-23-5 The foul will be on No. 3 if contact is made. When taking an initial defensive position in the path of the player who does not have the ball, time and distance must be sufficient to permit that player to stop or change his or her direction. When the player without the ball is moving rapidly, one step is not enough.

4-24-5 Defenders are not permitted to have hands on the dribbler or a player with the ball. Placing a hand on the offensive player more than once is a foul.

4-25-2 When the release of the airborne players try or pass is prevented by an opponent, it is a held ball. A held ball also occurs when opponents have their hands so firmly on the ball that neither can get control without roughness. An alternating-possession throw-in follows from the nearest out-of-bounds spot.

SCREENING PRINCIPLES

A screen is legal action by a player who, without causing contact, delays or prevents an opponent from reaching a desired position.

To establish a legal screening position, the screener may face any direction. Time and distance are relevant. The screener must be stationary, except when both are moving in the same path and direction. The screener must stay within his or her vertical plane with a stance approximately shoulder width apart.

When screening a stationary opponent from the front or side (within the visual field), the screener may be anywhere short of contact.

When screening a stationary opponent from behind (outside the visual field), the screener must allow the opponent one normal step backward without contact.

When screening a moving opponent, the screener must allow the opponent time and distance to avoid contact by stopping or changing direction. The speed of the player to be screened will determine where the screener may take his or her position. The position will vary and may be one to two normal steps or strides from the opponent.

When screening an opponent who is moving in the same path and direction as the screener, the player behind is responsible if contact is made because the player in front slows up or stops and the player behind overruns his or her opponent.

A player who is screened within his or her visual field is expected to avoid contact with the screener by stopping or going around the screener. In cases of screens outside the visual field, the opponent may make inadvertent contact with the screener and if the opponent is running rapidly, the contact may be severe. Such a case is to be ruled as incidental contact provided the opponent stops or attempts to stop on contact and moves around the screen, and provided the screener was not displaced if he or she has the ball.

The following illustrations should be reviewed carefully as they show examples of some common screening situations. The basic principles must be thoroughly studied so that players understand them and official's rulings are consistently accurate.

4-40 A new entry in the NFHS Casebook clarifies that a player standing on a boundary line cannot set a legal screen because he/she does not have legal position on the playing floor. PlayPic A shows a legal screen as the screener is inbounds with legal position.

4-40 In PlayPic B, the screener is on or outside the boundary line and is therefore not in a legal position to set a screen. Any illegal contact is a foul on the screener.

4-40-2 Number 12 fouls in (2) by stepping into No. 3's path as she attempts to go around the screen. The screener must be stationary and may not lean into the opponent or extend arms, elbows, hips, legs, etc. The screener must stay within his or her vertical plane with a stance approximately shoulder width apart. This illegal action is a team-control blocking foul on No. 12.

4-40-3 Number 12 screens at the side of stationary opponent No. 3. Number 12 is within No. 3's visual field and may be as close as she wishes without making contact. The defensive player can see the screen and, therefore, is expected to detour around it. The responsibility for contact is on No. 3.

4-40-3 Legal screen as No. 10 and No. 12 set the screen to the side of No. 3, and the dribbler breaks around the screen without making contact. Legal play as the screen was set to the side of the defender.

4-40-4 Even though screener No. 5 positions herself too close to No. 4 for her to take one normal step back, there is no foul because there was no contact. A player cannot be charged with an illegal screen, or a blocking foul unless there has been contact.

4-40-4 A player screened from behind is given additional protection by the rules. When a stationary player is screened from behind, the screened player must be able to take a normal step backward without contacting the screener. The player being screened is not expected to see a screen set outside his or her visual field. Number 4 will be able to turn and see the screener and can either stop or go around her.

4-40-5 A blocking foul on No. 15 who moved into the path of moving opponent No. 10 too late for him to stop or change direction. To set a screen on a moving opponent, the same principles on distance applies as when an initial guarding position is taken on a moving opponent without the ball. The opponent must be able to stop or change direction.

4-40-6 This is an example of a legal moving screen. There are not too many opportunities to use a legal moving screen. Number 10 may continue in the path he established at any speed he desires and any contact caused by No. 3 on No. 10 will be an illegal contact foul on No. 3.

4-40-8 The defender attempts to force his way between No. 12 and No. 10 when there is not enough room. This is a charging foul on the defender. The screened player must stop on contact and/or go around the screeners rather than try to fight through the screen.

4-41-1, 5, 6, 7 The player taps the ball toward his basket. The ball does not rest in the hand, but the hand is momentarily in contact with the ball in order to give it direction. In a tap for goal the player attempts to direct the ball into his basket.

4-41-1, 5, 6, 7 In this illustration, the tapper is fouled when the tapper's hand touches the ball. This is a foul in the act of shooting and results in one free throw as the tap was successful.

4-41-5, 8 The ball does not become dead when it is in the air on a tap even if time expires. A tap by a player toward his basket ends exactly as a try for goal ends and does not become dead if a foul occurs.

4-41-1, 5, 6, 7 The airborne shooter is fouled following the tap, but before returning to the floor. This is a foul in the act of shooting and either one or two free throws will be awarded depending on whether the tap is successful or unsuccessful.

4-41-1, 5, 6, 7 The player who tapped the ball is an airborne shooter and the contact in returning to the floor is a player-control foul. No goal can be scored whether or not the tapped ball goes through the basket.

4-42-3, 4, 5 The throw-in count is started properly in (1) when the throw-in begins. The throw-in count ends on release of the ball in (2). The count stops when the thrower releases the ball on a pass directly into the court. However, the throw-in does not end, and if stopped, the clock does not start, until the released ball touches or is touched by an inbounds player other than the thrower.

4-42-5 The throw-in ends when the passed ball touches or is touched by another player inbounds. The rule prevents the defensive team from committing a violation, especially during an alternating-possession throw-in.

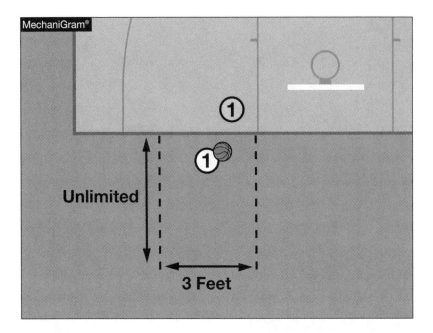

4-42-6 The thrower, when required to remain within the designated spot, may jump, pivot or shuffle their feet as long as a foot is kept on or above the 3-foot area. The thrower must keep one foot on or over the spot until the ball is released.

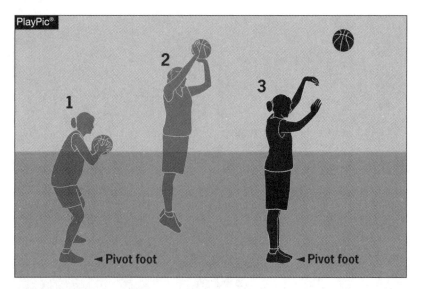

4-44-3 This player's right foot is her pivot foot. In (2), the player lifts the pivot foot, and the ball leaves her hand on a try before the pivot foot returns to the floor. This maneuver is legal.

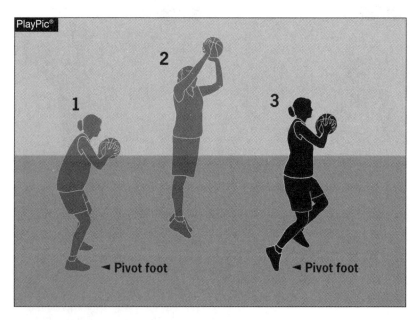

4-44-3 This player's right foot is her pivot foot. In (2),the player lifts the pivot foot, and jumps to shoot a jump shot. However, in (3), it is a traveling violation as the pivot foot returns to the floor before the ball leaves the player's hand on a try.

4-44-3 When the player, after jumping from the floor, drops the ball to the floor to avoid having the try blocked and then recovers or bounces the ball, it is a traveling violation. When she touches the ball, it is a violation as she released the ball to start a dribble with her pivot foot off the floor.

4-47-4 A team shall be issued a team warning for delay when it fails to have the court ready for play following a time-out. It is one of the four delay situations when a team will receive a team warning for delay.

4-48-1a In PlayPic A, the official shall stop the game and begin the administrative process to have the warning to the team bench recorded by the scorer in the scorebook and then notify the head coach. In PlayPic B, when the behavior is major no warning should be issued and the officials should rule a technical foul.

Plane violation warning

Interfering with ball after goal

Huddle with free thrower

4-47-1, 2, 3, 10-1-5 A team will receive only one team delay warning for any of the four delay situations. (The fourth delay situation, not having the court ready for play following a time-out, is pictured on the previous page.) Any subsequent delay in any of the four team delay categories will result in a team technical foul.

Part 3
Rule 5

Scoring and Timing Regulations

A goal is made when a live ball enters the basket from above and remains in the basket or passes through it. Even though the ball is live during a throw-in, no goal can be scored if the ball is thrown into the basket from out of bounds without first touching a player on the court. If a player-control foul occurs before or after a goal, the goal is canceled. A goal from the field counts two points for the team into whose basket the ball is thrown. A successful try or thrown ball from the field by a player located behind his or her 19-foot 9-inch line counts three points. A goal from a free throw is credited to the thrower and counts one point for his or her team.

The scorer shall record the field goals made, the free throws made and missed and keep a running score. Personal and technical fouls are recorded. An official is notified whenever a player is charged with a fifth foul (personal and technical) or second technical foul. The scorer records charged time-outs and notifies the coach through an official when a team has used its allotted time-outs in regulation. These are but a few of the major duties the scorer must perform. A complete listing of duties can be found on the "Instruction Sheet for the Scorer" produced by the NFHS.

The timer shall note when each half is to start and shall notify the referee more than three minutes before this time so that the referee may notify or have the teams notified. The timer shall signal the scorer three minutes before starting time. The timer shall start or stop the clock as provided in the rules. This includes a warning signal before the expiration of an intermission or charged time-out. A complete listing of duties can be found on the "Instruction Sheet for the Timer" produced by the NFHS.

5-1-2 After No. 4 releases the ball on the dunk, he becomes an airborne shooter. The subsequent contact is a player-control foul. The foul cancels the goal, even though the ball was through the basket and dead when the foul occurred. Team B is given the ball for a designated-spot throw-in at the out-of-bounds spot nearest to where the foul occurred.

5-2-5 The throw-in is made with three-tenths (.3) of a second on the clock. The throw-in pass is caught by No. 3 and he then tries for goal. No goal can be scored on a try whether or not the ball is in flight on the try when time expires. In this situation only a tap could score.

5-4-1 The coach has already been charged with a technical foul for failure to replace a disqualified player with a substitute available. It would serve no purpose to repeat the penalty or disqualify the coach. In this situation, the referee has support and authority to forfeit the game. Any act which makes a travesty of the game may result in forfeiture. However, a game should not be forfeited for the action of spectators.

5-6-2 Exception 1 The legal touching by No. 2 does not cause the try to end — thus the goal counts in (1) and (2) as the ball was in flight prior to the expiration of time. If No. 2's touching had been goaltending, it would have caused the ball to become dead.

5-6-2 Exception 3 A foul occurs as time expires in the fourth quarter. Team B leads by two points. In (2), when A5 misses the first free throw, the second free throw is not attempted as the winner of the game has been determined.

5-8-3 Only the players currently in the game or the head coach may request a time-out. The official shall see/hear the time-out request from either a player or head coach. If no indication is made for a 30-second time-out, then a 60-second time-out shall be charged.

5-8-3 In PlayPic A, the official incorrectly grants a time-out without player control. When a secondary official sees or hears a request for a time-out, that official needs to ensure the ball status prior to granting a time-out. In PlayPic B, the official correctly does not grant a time-out with player-control status unknown. In PlayPic C, the officials ensure player-control status prior to granting the timeout.

5-10-1 When the foul occurs with 2.6 seconds left in (1), the clock will be reset to 2.6 seconds in (2) when the official has definite knowledge. The need for lag time or reaction time by the clock operator has been eliminated.

4-43-2 In (1) the coach decides to request a 30-second time-out. In (2) the coach decides to request a 60-second time-out and the official properly instructs the scorer to also charge a 60-second time-out which begins immediately upon expiration of the 30-second time-out.

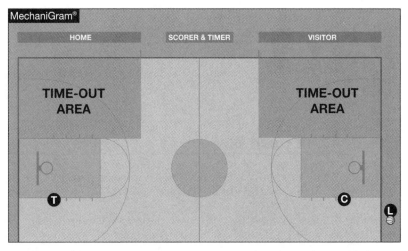

5-11-2, 5-11-3, 1-13-3 Time-outs shall be conducted within the confines of the time-out area. Players shall remain standing during a 30-second time-out.

5-11-7 In no case shall successive charged time-outs be granted after playing time has expired in the fourth quarter or any overtime period. Team B's request is denied. This prohibition applies to one team or a single time-out by one team followed by a request by the opponents. In the case of expired time, the next opportunity for a time-out by either team occurs only after the clock has run in the overtime period.

Part 3
Rule 6

Live Ball and Dead Ball

Accurate rules enforcement is very often dependent on a clear understanding of exactly when the ball becomes dead and when it becomes live.

When the ball is dead, there are only three ways by which it can become live. These are:

1. When the ball leaves the tossing official's hand on a jump ball.
2. When, on a free throw, the ball is at the disposal of the free thrower.
3. When, on a throw-in, the ball is at the disposal of the thrower.

Unless there is continuous motion or the ball is in flight during a try or tap, the whistle always causes the ball to become dead if it is not already dead. The whistle is nearly always used merely as a convenient method of attracting attention to something which has already occurred to cause the ball to become dead.

Some rules fundamentals which apply are:

1. While the ball remains live, a loose ball always remains in control of the team whose player last had control, unless it is loose on a try for goal.
2. Neither a team nor any player is in control during a dead ball, or during a jump ball or when the ball is in flight during a try or tap for goal.
3. Any free-throw violation by the offense causes the ball to become dead immediately.
4. A live-ball foul by the offense (team in control), or the expiration of time for a quarter/period, causes the ball to become dead immediately, unless the ball is in flight during a tap or try for goal. The ball also becomes dead immediately if the airborne shooter commits a player-control foul.

6-1-1 The game and each extra period shall be started by a jump ball in the center restraining circle by the designated official. Thereafter, play shall be resumed by a jump ball, a throw-in or by placing it at the disposal of a free thrower. Any two opponents may jump to start the game and each extra period. A throw-in under the alternating-possession procedure will start the second, third and fourth quarters and be administered by the referee.

6-1-2b The ball is at the disposal of the thrower when it is available to him. The official has properly started the throw-in count and the ball is live. Anytime the ball is accessible to the thrower and all he or she needs to do is pick it up, the throw-in count shall be started.

6-3-5a Team A's No. 3 breaks the plane of the center restraining-circle cylinder after the ball is touched by a jumper. This is not a violation. Nonjumpers may move off the circle at any time. After the toss they may change positions around the circle or move into unoccupied spaces.

6-4-1 Number 3 controls the ball then fumbles it out of bounds. Team B is awarded the ball for a throw-in because of the violation. The arrow is set immediately as Team A did obtain momentary control of the ball following the jump. This means Team B also gets the possession arrow and will have the first alternating-possession throw-in when the next jump ball or held ball occurs.

6-4-3 NOTE The opening jump ball (1) results in a held ball between Nos. 22 and 34 (2). Since alternating possession has not been established, a jump ball will occur between Nos. 22 and 34 (3) in the center restraining circle.

6-4-4 A held ball in (1) results in an alternating-possession throw-in for Team B in (2). The possession arrow is properly reversed when the throw-in ends. Team A will have the next opportunity when an alternating-possession throw-in results.

6-7-4 While airborne, No. 4 taps the ball toward his own basket. In returning to the floor, he fouls No. 5 who had legal position before No. 4 became airborne. The goal does not count as No. 4 is an airborne shooter on a tap. The foul is a player-control foul and Team B's throw-in will be from a designated spot on the end line.

6-7-7 Exception a The goal counts when tapper, No. 4, is fouled after he taps the ball as the foul did not cause the ball to become dead. Since the tap was successful, No. 4 is awarded one free throw as he was an airborne shooter when he was fouled.

6-7-7 Exception c This is continuous motion, and the try for field goal will count if made. Number 32 is awarded one free throw if the goal is made and two free throws if it is missed. The continuous-motion exception is the only situation when a foul before the ball is in flight on a try does not cause the ball to become dead immediately. The try for goal must have started before the opponent fouls in order for the continuous motion exception to apply.

Part 3
Rule 7

Out of Bounds and the Throw-in

The ball is out of bounds when it touches or is touched by any of the following which are out of bounds:
1. A player or any other person.
2. The floor or any object on or outside a boundary.
3. The supports or back of the backboard.
4. The ceiling or overhead equipment or supports.
5. A dribbler who is touching a boundary.

A player is out of bounds when he or she touches the floor or any object on or outside a boundary line. The location of an airborne player is the same as it was when he or she was last in contact with the floor.

The ball is caused to go out of bounds by the last player in bounds to touch it or to be touched by it, unless the ball touches a player who is out of bounds prior to touching something out of bounds other than a player. When a player bats the ball out of an opponent's hands and it goes out of bounds, the player who batted the ball caused it to go out.

The throw-in starts and the ball becomes live when the ball is at the disposal of a player entitled to the throw-in. The ball shall be released on a pass directly into the court within five seconds. The throw-in, except after a score or awarded score, must be made from a designated spot. The privilege of moving along the end line following a goal or awarded goal remains after a time-out, after a delay warning on the opponents and if a common foul or violation by the opponents occurs when the end-line privilege is in effect.

7-1-1 Number 3, who is dribbling, comes into contact with an opponent who is out of bounds. Number 3 has not violated, and the ball remains live. Number 3 is out of bounds if she touches the floor or an object (not a person) on or outside a boundary. Number 5 is a player and not an object. However, if the dribbler touches a boundary line, the ball is out of bounds.

7-1-1; 4-15-5 A player who is dribbling (player control) and steps out of bounds during the dribble, even though she is not touching the ball at the time, has violated.

7-5-1 The final horn has sounded in (1) indicating the halftime intermission is over, but Team A delays at its bench. The official properly places the ball on the floor and begins the five-second throw-in count in (2).

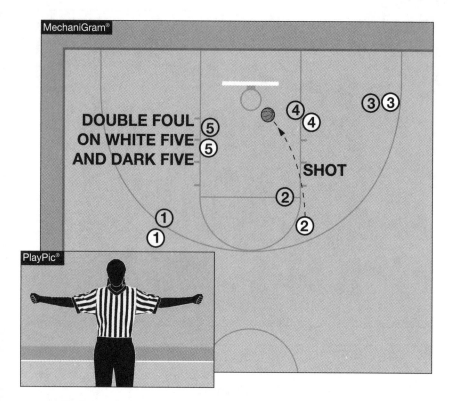

DOUBLE FOUL ON WHITE FIVE AND DARK FIVE

SHOT

7-5-3b The ball is in flight on a try by A when A5 and B5 commit double flagrant personal fouls. Both players are ejected, no free throws are awarded and play is resumed at the point of interruption. If the try is successful, the point of interruption is a throw-in by the non-scoring team from anywhere along the end line. If the try is unsuccessful, the team entitled to the ball under the alternating-possession procedure will have a throw-in at a designated spot nearest to where the ball was located when the fouls occurred.

7-5-4 A foul by Team A occurs before the free-throw attempt is in flight in (1). The lane is cleared. Since the free throw was missed in (2), the throw-in for Team B is from the spot out of bounds nearest the foul in (3). If the last free throw had been successful, the throw-in would have been from anywhere outside the end line. This is a team-control foul.

7-5-7 Goaltending occurs and a dead-ball player-control foul is committed in (2). Team A is awarded two points for the goaltending violation. Since the player-control foul in (2) does not result in a free throw for No. 5, Team B is allowed to move along the end line because of the awarded goal.

7-5-7 When there is a score, more than one player of the scored-upon team may be out of bounds outside the end line. Number 10 grabs the ball after the score, passes it to teammate No. 4, and is moving onto the court when No. 4 makes the throw-in. A player may move along the end line before making a throw-in following a goal or awarded goal. There is no limit on the number of passes which may be made outside the end line provided a five-second count is not reached.

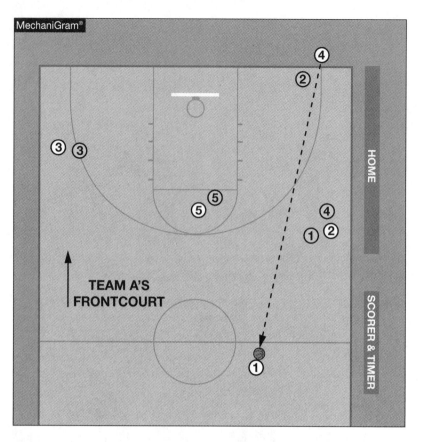

7-6-2 Number 4 passes the ball from out of bounds outside the end line to his/her teammate in the backcourt. That is legal as the ball does not have either frontcourt or backcourt status during a throw-in. Once the ball is controlled in the backcourt, Team A will have 10 seconds to advance the ball to A's frontcourt.

7-6-4; 9-2-10 Penalty 3,4; 10-3-10 It is a technical foul in (1) when the defender reaches through the boundary plane and touches or slaps the ball away. In (2) it is an intentional personal foul when the defender contacts the thrower. If Team B has not previously been warned for reaching through the boundary plane, the foul also constitutes the warning being issued and recorded.

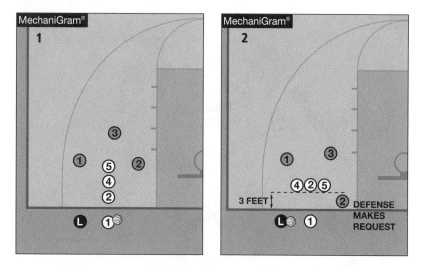

7-6-5 In (1), teammates have legally lined up for a throw-in using a tandem formation, and are not required to allow an opponent to take a position between them. In (2), the opponent may take a position between the players who have lined up side by side at a distance within three feet from the end line and parallel to it. If the Team B player desires a position between the Team A players, he or she must make the request before the ball is at the disposal of the thrower.

7-6-6 When the ball is awarded to the wrong team, the mistake must be rectified before the throw-in ends. In (1), the mistake can be rectified. In (2), since the throw-in legally touched a player on the court the throw-in has ended and the mistake cannot be rectified.

Part 3
Rule 8

Free Throw

A free throw is the opportunity given a player to score one point by an unhindered try for goal from within the free-throw semicircle and behind the free-throw line. The try for goal shall be made within 10 seconds after the ball has been placed at the disposal of the free thrower at the free-throw line.

The free throw(s) awarded because of a personal foul shall be attempted by the offended player. If the offended player is injured or disqualified, his or her substitute shall attempt the free throws. Technical-foul free throws may be attempted by any player(s), including an entering substitute of the offended team.

The three spaces on each side of the lane beginning at the end line and moving toward the free-throw line are designated as marked lane spaces. The three marked lane spaces on each side of the lane are the only spaces which may be occupied. Except for the free thrower, all other players must either be in marked spaces or behind the free-throw line extended and behind the three-point line.

During a free throw for a personal foul, other than intentional or flagrant, each of the marked lane spaces adjacent to the end line shall be occupied by one opponent of the free thrower unless the resumption-of-play procedure is in effect following a time-out or intermission. A teammate of the free thrower is entitled to the next adjacent marked lane space on each side. No more than one player may occupy any part of a marked lane space. Only four defensive and two offensive players are permitted in marked lane spaces. If the ball is to become dead when the last free throw for a specific penalty is not successful, players shall not take positions along the free-throw lane line.

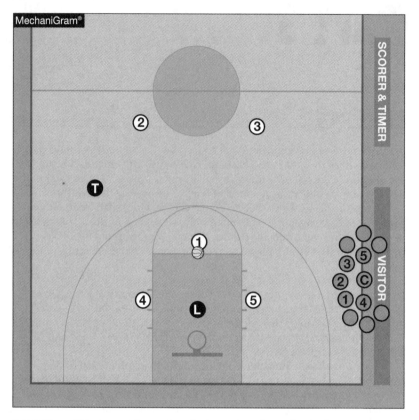

8-1-2 Team B is not ready to play during a free throw by A after a time-out. Following the necessary signals, the administering official uses the resumption-of-play procedure and puts the ball at the free thrower's disposal. Since Team B is not occupying the first marked space on each side, it is an automatic violation by B if the throw is missed. If B does violate in this situation, any further delay in occupying the spaces during the substitute throw would result in a technical foul.

8-1-4; 8-1-5 If the ball is to remain live when the last free throw for a specific penalty is not successful, opponents of the free thrower shall occupy the lane space nearest the end line on both sides of the lane unless the resumption-of-play procedure is in effect following a time-out or intermission. Teammates of the free thrower are entitled to the second lane space. A team forfeits its right to any of the entitled spaces after the ball is at the free-thrower's disposal.

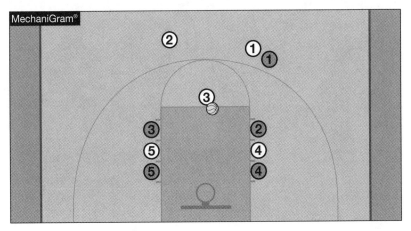

MechaniGram®

8-1-4b, c, d, e The defensive players shall assume the first space on the lane line. That leaves the area between the end line and the first lane-space mark vacant. A lane-space mark (2 inches by 8 inches) must be applied to the lane line near the free-throw line to designate the last 3-foot marked lane space.

8-3 The free throws awarded for a technical foul may be attempted by any player, including an incoming substitute. The coach or captain shall designate the free thrower. Since an individual technical foul results in two free throws, each free throw may be attempted by a different player. If a technical foul occurs before the game starts, a substitute(s) may take the place of a designated starter to attempt the free throws.

8-3 The pregame dunk in (1) dictates the game will begin with the administration of the free throws. In (2), No. 11 who was not designated to start, legally enters to attempt one or both of the free throws. The replaced starter may not return until after the clock has run following the last free throw.

8-6-2 The ball is live and at the disposal of Team A in (1). This is a continuous-motion foul. If No. 2 was in the habitual motion of shooting the ball, the free-throw attempt counts and is successful if made. The penalties are administered in the order in which the fouls occurred. Team A No. 13 will then attempt a bonus free throw in (2) as a result of the foul committed by Team B No. 22 in (1).

8-6-2, 8-6-3 In (1), a shooting foul on No. 55 has occurred. In (2), a subsequent double technical foul is ruled on Nos. 40 and 21. In (3), play resumes with the free throws for the shooting foul, as if the double technical foul had not occurred.

Part 3
Rule 9

Violations and Penalties

An infraction in basketball is simply an act of breaking one of the game rules. Whenever an infraction occurs, it is either a violation or a foul. It is often assumed that a violation is a minor infraction since no free throws are awarded. However, loss of the ball to opponents or awarding of points because of basket interference or goaltending can be very costly. Violations are of three types.

1. Free-throw violations.
2. Floor violations.
3. Basket interference and goaltending.

Free-Throw Violations

This violation causes the ball to become dead immediately if it is by the free throwing team; but if it is by its opponent, it is a delayed dead ball since the ball remains live until the free throw ends. If the free thrower or his or her teammate violates, no goal can be scored. If the opponent violates, it results in a substitute free throw if the attempt is not successful. If both teams violate simultaneously, no goal can be scored, and unless another free throw follows, a throw-in is awarded under the alternating-possession procedure. If an opponent violates, followed by a teammate of the free thrower in a marked lane space, the second violation is ignored.

Floor Violations

A floor violation — like a 10-second backcourt violation or a throw-in violation — causes the ball to become dead. The penalty is the awarding of the ball to the opponents at the out-of-bounds spot nearest the violation. The more common floor violations include traveling, free-throw lane, backcourt, closely guarded, and those involving a throw-in.

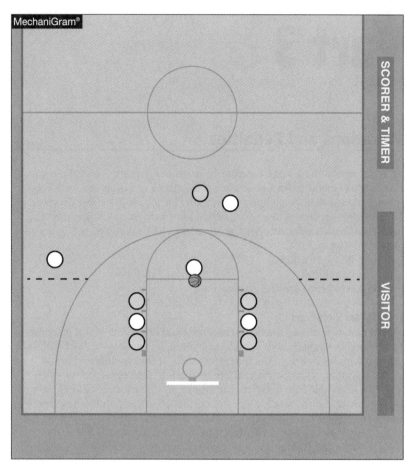

9-1-3a A player, other than the free thrower, who does not occupy a marked lane space, may not have either foot beyond the vertical plane of the free-throw line extended and three-point line which is farther from the basket, until the ball touches the ring or until the free throw ends.

9-9-1 An exception has been added to the rule to clarify that any player located in the backcourt may recover a ball deflected from the frontcourt by the defense even if the ball has not touched in the backcourt following the deflection, as shown in the PlayPic.

9-9-1 It was already legal for a player to be the first to touch the ball in the backcourt if it was last touched in the frontcourt by a player on the opposing team and had obtained backcourt status before the recovery.

9-1-3b-g Free-throw restrictions apply for players along marked lane spaces until the ball is released by the free thrower; and for the free thrower or players outside of marked lane spaces until the ball touches the ring or backboard or the free throw ends.

9-1-3d A free-throw violation has occurred when a player contacts any part of the court outside the marked lane space (three feet by three feet).

ENTERS
LANE EARLY

9-1-3d; 9-1 Penalty 1 A teammate of the free thrower commits a free-throw violation by leaving a marked lane space prematurely. The violation causes the ball to become dead immediately and cancels the attempt. Unless another free throw follows, play resumes with a designated spot throw-in by Team B.

9-1 Penalty 4 If a defensive player in a marked lane space violates followed by a teammate of the free thrower (also in a marked lane space), only the first violation is penalized.

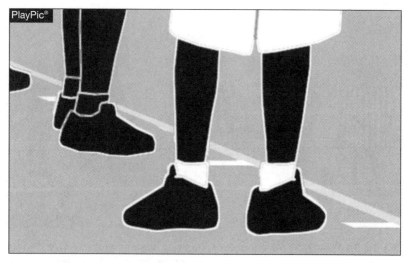

9-1-3g A player occupying a marked lane space must have one foot positioned near the outer edge of the free-throw lane line with the other positioned anywhere within the designated 36-inch lane space.

9-1-3h Players occupying marked free-throw lane line spaces may not enter the free-throw semicircle until the ball touches the ring or until the free throw ends.

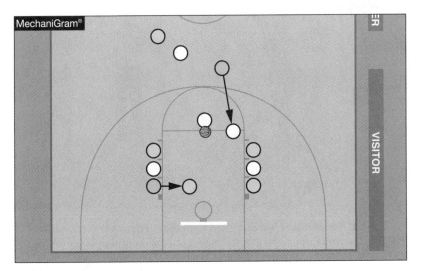

9-1 Penalties 4b If there is a violation first by the free thrower's opponent followed by the free thrower or a teammate: If the second violation is by the free thrower or a teammate behind the free-throw line extended and/or the three-point line, both violations are penalized, as in penalty item 3.

9-2-2 In (1), No. 10 commits a throw-in violation when the throw-in pass strikes the floor out of bounds. In (2), it is not a violation when No. 4 bounces the ball on the out-of-bounds area before making the throw-in.

9-2-2; 9-3-2 The thrower has complied with requirements by passing the ball into the court from out of bounds so it touches another player on the court who is either inbounds or out of bounds. Number 3 violates when she touches the throw-in pass while touching out of bounds. The ensuing throw-in will be for Team A from the location where number 3 violated.

9-2-3 It is a throw-in violation by Team A when a Team A player touches her throw-in pass while the ball is on the out-of-bounds side of the throw-in boundary plane. The ball is awarded for a throw-in to Team B at the original throw-in spot.

9-2-10 Penalty 4 When an opponent contacts the thrower-in, an intentional foul shall be charged to the offender.

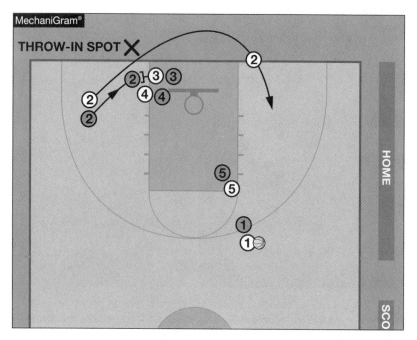

9-3-3 A2 goes out of bounds along the end line to take advantage of a low screen set by teammates. A violation is ruled on A2 as soon as that player goes out of bounds. Team B is awarded a designated spot throw-in nearest to where the violation occurred.

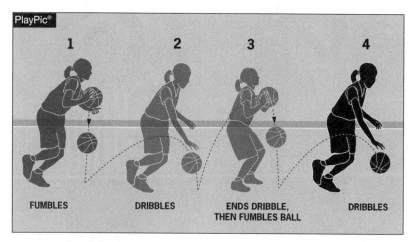

1 FUMBLES **2** DRIBBLES **3** ENDS DRIBBLE, THEN FUMBLES BALL **4** DRIBBLES

9-5-3 The player gains control after the fumble and dribbles. She ends the dribble and then fumbles again. She could recover the ball, but it is a violation in (4) to dribble again. A player is in control and cannot travel during a dribble.

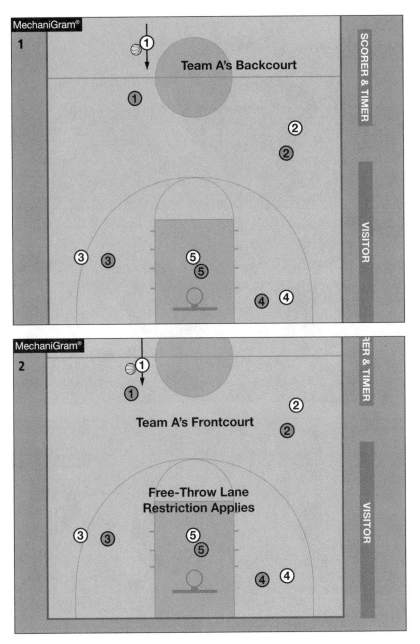

9-7-1 The free-throw lane restriction is not in effect while the ball is in Team A's backcourt as in (1) or during a throw-in. The three-second restriction applies only when the ball is in A's frontcourt and only while Team A is in control as in (2) (also includes an interrupted dribble).

9-8 Violation. A team shall not be in continuous team control in its backcourt for more than 10 seconds. Team control was not lost by the dribbler when the ball was batted by the opponent even though the dribble ended. The count continues, and it becomes a violation when the count of 10 is reached.

9-9-1 In (1), the player with her pivot foot (right foot) in the backcourt can pivot the left foot into the frontcourt and then to the backcourt in (2) without committing a violation. In (3), the player uses her front foot or left foot as her pivot foot and pivots into the frontcourt. However, when she now touches the backcourt in (4), it would be a violation.

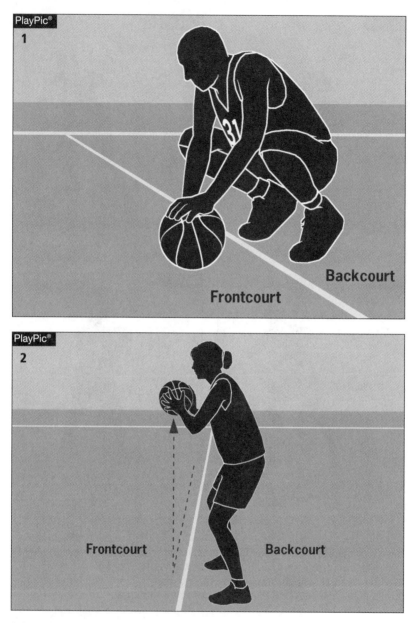

PlayPic®
1

Backcourt

Frontcourt

PlayPic®
2

Frontcourt

Backcourt

9-9-1 The division line is in the backcourt. In (1), the ball remains in the backcourt even though the player touches the ball to the floor in the frontcourt. This is not a violation. In (2), when the player dribbles the ball while in the backcourt, it remains in the backcourt until the ball and both feet of the dribbler touch entirely in the frontcourt. There has been no violation. The 10-second count continues.

Backcourt **Frontcourt**

9-9-1 The ball has not been to the backcourt, since it has not touched the backcourt or anyone in it. While in the air, No. 4's location is the frontcourt.

A'S BACKCOURT **A'S FRONTCOURT**

9-9-1 A player shall not be the first to touch the ball after it has been in team control in the frontcourt, or if he/she or a teammate last touched or was touched by the ball in the frontcourt before it went to the backcourt.

A's Backcourt   A's Frontcourt

9-9-1 During a throw-in, No. 4 passes the ball to No. 10 in the frontcourt. No. 10 muffs the ball and it goes into the backcourt. It is not a violation for No. 10 to recover the ball in A's backcourt as Team A has not established control in its frontcourt. Player and team control are established in the backcourt when No. 10 secures control of the ball.

Frontcourt   Backcourt

9-9-2 A violation occurs when a player causes the ball to go from backcourt to frontcourt and return untouched to backcourt if he or she or a teammate is first to touch the ball.

9-9-3 In (1), the player leaps from the backcourt while the ball has already obtained frontcourt status by No. 3. In (2), the player catches the ball while airborne and lands in the frontcourt in (3). This is a backcourt violation as the previous location of the player who caught the ball in the air was the backcourt.

9-9-3 On a throw-in, if a player of either team is first to gain control while airborne, no violation occurs if the player jumped from frontcourt (1) and lands in backcourt (2). The same provision is in effect for both teams during a jump ball.

9-9-3 When the ball is touched on a throw-in by the opposing team, the throw-in has legally ended. Since a throw-in exception cannot apply, when the offensive player takes off from the frontcourt (1) and lands in the backcourt (2), a backcourt violation has occurred.

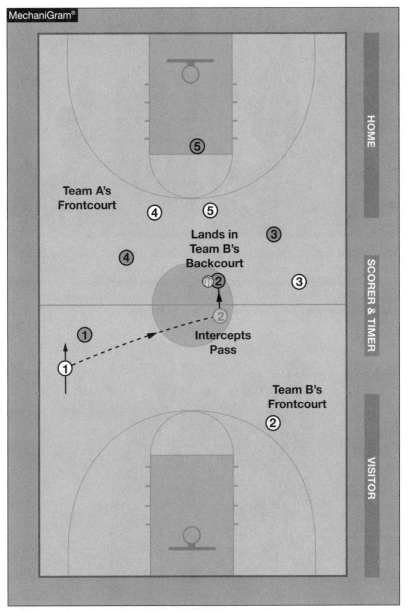

Team A's
Frontcourt

Lands in
Team B's
Backcourt

Intercepts
Pass

Team B's
Frontcourt

9-9-3 B2, while airborne, intercepts a pass from A1 to A3. B2 had jumped from Team B's frontcourt and landed in Team B's backcourt. This is not a violation. The provision is provided only to the defensive team and only to the player who secures control while airborne.

9-10-1a The trail official properly gives a closely guarded count in (1) and then begins a closely guarded dribble count in (2) when No. 3 begins to dribble. The dribble count continues as long as the closely guarded situation exists anywhere in the frontcourt. The official should switch arms when going directly from one counting situation to another.

9-10-1b If players use the sideline or end line to keep an opponent from reaching the ball for five seconds a violation will be ruled. If one or more opponents are within six feet of the ball or screening players and cannot get to the ball because of the boundary line or the players, a closely guarded situation is in effect.

BASKET INTERFERENCE AND GOALTENDING

Either of these violations causes the ball to become dead, and either may occur at the offender's basket or at the opponent's basket. The try for a field goal or free throw can never be successful if basket interference or goaltending occurs, however, compensating points may be awarded as penalty for the infraction.

If the ball did not become dead when the violation occurred, it would be necessary to credit the offending player with a field goal in the wrong basket when the violation is at the opponent's basket. It would be even more of a problem in the case of a free throw. The awarding or canceling of point(s) is easily administered after the ball is dead.

Basket interference can occur during either a field-goal attempt or a free-throw attempt. It is basket interference to touch the ball or basket when the ball is on or within either basket, to touch the ball when it is touching the cylinder above the ring, to touch the ball outside the cylinder while reaching through the basket from below, or to pull down a movable ring so that it contacts the ball before the ring returns to its original position. If an opponent interferes, either two or three points will be awarded depending on whether it was a two- or three-point try. One point is awarded during a free-throw attempt, if a teammate interferes, no points can be scored.

Goaltending applies either during a free throw, or a try or tap in flight. Goaltending is touching the ball during a field goal try or touching a tapped ball which is in its downward flight entirely above the basket ring level and has the possibility of entering the basket in flight. If an opponent goaltends, two or three points are awarded depending on whether it was a two- or three-point attempt. If the offense goaltends, no points can be scored. Goaltending occurs during a free-throw attempt if the ball is touched by an opponent of the free thrower after being released and while it is outside the cylinder. Goaltending by the defense during a free throw is a technical foul in addition to the violation. One point is awarded if an opponent violates.

9-11; 4-6 While the ball is on Team B's basket, a player of Team B commits basket interference at his team's basket by touching the ball while it is on the ring. The ball becomes dead immediately and no points can be scored. The ball is awarded to Team A for a throw-in at the out-of-bounds spot nearest the violation.

9-11; 4-6 This is basket interference by a Team B player during a field-goal try by a Team A player at A's basket. Team A is awarded two points when the interference occurs during a two-point try and three points if during a three-point try. The official hands or bounces the ball to a Team B player for a throw-in anywhere along the end line nearest Team A's basket.

9-11; 4-6 It is a basket-interference violation for either the offense or defense to touch the net when the ball is on or within the basket. The violation causes the ball to become dead. If Team B interferes, Team A is awarded one point if it occurs during a free-throw try and two or three points in case of a two- or three-point try respectively. If Team A interferes, no points can be scored, and the ball is awarded out of bounds to Team B at the nearest spot.

9-11; 4-6 Number 4 touches the ball during a field goal try while it is in the cylinder above his basket and taps it into the basket. This is offensive basket interference. No goal. It is Team B's ball for a throw-in at the nearest spot out of bounds.

9-11; 4-6 Exception Number 4 secures a rebound while the ball is clearly outside the cylinder. As he jumps to dunk the ball into his basket in (1), No. 55 in blocking the shot places his hand against the ball while both the ball and the hand of player No. 55 are clearly outside the cylinder. In (2), No. 4 forces the ball and the hand of No. 55 into the cylinder. There is no violation by either player and a held ball with alternating-possession results.

9-11; 9-12 This block is legal as the ball is still in its upward flight and is not in the imaginary cylinder above the ring when touched by the defender. If the ball had been in its downward flight outside the cylinder and had a chance of entering the basket, it would have been defensive goaltending, if the touching had occurred with the ball in or touching the cylinder, it would have been basket interference.

9-12 Number 45 is goaltending whether it is a tap or try at Team A's basket. There is no difference in a tap or try as it applies to goaltending. The offended team is awarded two points on a two-point try and three points on a three-point try. Goaltending cannot occur on a field-goal attempt unless the ball has a chance of entering the basket in flight.

9-13 A violation in both (1) and (2). In (1), the violation does not cause the ball to become dead until the try is made or missed, then the violation is penalized. If the violation had been by the offense while the try was in flight, the ball would have been dead immediately. In (2), the ball is dead immediately. If contact occurs it would be either a player-control, intentional or flagrant foul.

Part 3
Rule 10

Fouls and Penalties

Personal fouls involve contact during a live ball, except when committed by or on an airborne shooter. Technical fouls do not normally involve contact, but generally occur during a dead-ball period with the clock stopped.

The penalty for a foul is usually the awarding of one, two or three unhindered free throws and/or the ball for a throw-in to a player of the offended team. Penalties for fouls also include the offender being charged with the foul in the scorebook. Disqualification results upon being charged with a flagrant foul, a fifth foul or second technical foul.

PENALTY TECHNICAL FOUL: Specific infractions may be committed by a team, player, substitute, bench personnel or coach.

The penalty for a single technical foul is two free throws plus the ball for a throw-in at the division line opposite the table. If the foul is flagrant, the offender is disqualified. A technical foul on bench personnel for unsporting conduct carries not only the two free throw penalty but in addition all such "bench" fouls are charged to the offender and also charged indirectly to the head coach. The second technical foul charged to a player, team member or any bench personnel, other than the head coach, results in disqualification. The third technical foul or the second technical foul charged directly to the head coach results in disqualification.

If a player, team member or other bench personnel commits a flagrant foul, the offender is disqualified to the bench. The same disqualification of a coach or adult bench personnel results in ejection from the building, or the offender must go to the team's locker room.

PENALTY PERSONAL FOUL: Offender is charged with one foul, and if it is his or her fifth foul (personal and technical), or if it is flagrant, he or she is disqualified. The offended player is awarded free throws as follows:

Summary of Penalties for All Fouls
The offended player or team is awarded the following:
1. No free throws:
   a. For each common foul before the bonus rule is in effect.
   b. For a player-control or team-control foul.
   c. For double personal or technical fouls (point of interruption).
   d. For simultaneous personal or technical fouls by opponents (point of interruption).
   e. After time has expired for the fourth quarter (or extra period), unless the point(s) would affect the outcome of the game.

NOTE: If one or both fouls of a double personal foul are flagrant, no free throws are awarded. Any player who commits a flagrant foul is disqualified.

2. One free throw if fouled in the act of shooting and the two- or three-point try or tap is successful.

3. Bonus free throw:
   a. For seventh, eighth and ninth team foul each half, if first free throw is successful.
   b. Beginning with 10th team foul each half whether or not first free throw is successful.

4. Two free throws if intentional or flagrant, plus ball for throw-in.

5. Fouled in act of shooting and try or tap is unsuccessful:
   a. Two free throws on two-point try or tap.
   b. Three free throws on three-point try or tap. Plus ball for throw-in if intentional or flagrant.

6. Multiple Foul:
   a. One free throw for each foul:
      1. No try involved.
      2. Successful or unsuccessful two-point try or tap.
      3. Successful three-point try or tap.
   b. Two free throws for each foul:
      1. Intentional or flagrant foul.
      2. Unsuccessful three-point try or tap.
   Plus ball for throw-in if intentional or flagrant.
   NOTE: If one or both fouls of a multiple foul are flagrant, two free throws are awarded for each flagrant foul. Any player who commits a flagrant foul is disqualified.

7. In case of a false double foul or a false multiple foul, each foul carries its own penalty.

8. Fighting:
   a. Players on the court:
      1. Corresponding number from each team - double flagrant fouls, all participants are disqualified, no free throws are awarded, ball is put in play at the point of interruption.
      2. Numbers of participants are not corresponding - Flagrant fouls and disqualification for all participants, two free throws are awarded for the offended team for each additional player, offended team awarded a division line throw in.
   b. Bench personnel, except the head coach, leaving bench area during a fight or when a fight may break out:
      1. Do NOT participate in the fight — all bench personnel leaving bench are assessed flagrant fouls and disqualified, the head coach is assessed a maximum of one indirect technical foul (regardless of the number leaving the bench). If the number of each team's offenders is corresponding, no free throws are awarded, and the ball is put in

play at the point of interruption. If the number of each team's offenders is unequal, a maximum of two free throws are awarded the offended team, followed by a division line throw-in opposite the table.

(2) Participate in the fight — all participants are assessed flagrant fouls and disqualified. The head coach is assessed one indirect technical foul for each bench personnel participating in the fight. If the number of each team's participants is corresponding, no free throws are awarded, and the ball is put in play at the point of interruption. If the number of each team's participants is unequal, two free throws are awarded the offended team for each additional participant, followed by a division line throw-in opposite the table.

NOTE: All fouls (except an indirect technical foul charged to the head coach) count toward the team's foul count in the half.

We'd like to make 11 a starter

10-1; 10-2 Administrative technical fouls are team fouls resulting in the administration of two free throws and the ball at the opposite division line for a throw-in. The head coach does not lose the opportunity to stand in the coaching box due to an administrative technical foul being assessed.

10-1-3 The coach is using a cellular phone at courtside for coaching purposes during a game, which is permitted.

10-1-3 A team shall not use a megaphone, any mechanical sounding device or electronic equipment for voice communication with players on the court. A team shall not use television monitors, replay equipment or computers to review a ruling of the game officials.

10-1-5d The official is ready to administer the second free throw, but three Team B players are huddling in the lane. In (2), the official properly instructs the scorer to record a team warning for delay. The warning is then announced to the coach. If Team B is issued another team warning for any type of delay, it will result in a technical foul.

10-4-2 (1) and (2) illustrate a player completing a throw-in but then waiting to step inbounds. In (3), A2 steps in and receives the pass. A technical foul shall be ruled when a player purposely and/or deceitfully delays his or her return to the court after legally being out of bounds.

10-4-3 Any player may grasp the basket to prevent possible injury. In the case shown, the offensive player is not penalized for grasping the ring to prevent injury to himself or to the defender. However, if such grasping causes basket interference, the interference is penalized.

10-4-4 The purpose of the rule is to penalize intentional or deliberate contact with the backboard with a technical foul. Contact that occurs incidentally in playing the game is permitted.

10-4-4 A player shall not: 1) place a hand on the backboard or ring to gain an advantage; or 2) intentionally slap or strike the backboard or cause the ring to vibrate, while a try or tap is in flight or is touching the backboard or is in the basket or imaginary cylinder above the basket.

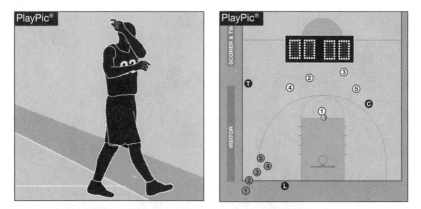

10-4-6i; 10-6-5 A player leaving the court for an unauthorized reason to show resentment, disgust or intimidation demonstrates unsporting behaviors by a player with a technical foul penalty assessed. In addition, a similar rule was added requiring team members to remain on the court and in the bench area while the game is in progress until each quarter or extra period has officially ended.

10-4-8 Penalty In (1), No. 2 commits a flagrant technical foul for fighting. In (2), he is disqualified and directed to go to Team B's bench. In (3), No. 2 remains under the supervision of the coach and jurisdiction of the officials.

10-4-10; 9-2 Penalty 3 A player who reaches through the throw-in boundary plane and touches or dislodges the ball commits a technical foul whether or not a throw-in plane warning had been given previously. This specific act is a player technical foul. The offended team will receive two free throws and the ball for a division-line throw-in.

10-5-5 Note 1) The head coach may enter the court to diffuse a situation where a fight may break out or has broken out to prevent it from escalating. 2) Assistant coaches or other bench personnel who enter the court will be charged with flagrant technical fouls and disqualified.

10-6-1a The coaching-box rule is in effect by state association adoption. When the coaching box is not in effect, coaches are also restricted in their actions.

10-6-2 The timer shall start the 15-second clock and sound the warning horn immediately when the official notifies him or her to do so. The coach has 15 seconds to replace the disqualified player without penalty.

10-6-4 A maximum of one technical foul is charged directly to the head coach when a participant wears an illegal jersey, illegal pants/skirt or an illegal number. If the game is played in a state which utilizes the optional coaching box, the coach should be informed that he/she has lost the privilege of using the coaching box for the entire game.

10-7 Penalty 4 Number 5 is charged with a flagrant personal foul in (1) and is disqualified in (2). Number 20 is awarded two free throws whether or not the goal was successful. Players are not allowed in spaces along the lane during the free throws. In addition, Team A is awarded the ball for a throw-in at the out-of-bounds spot nearest to the foul.

10-7-1 Officials must recognize rough play and quickly take action to limit it. Excessive actions when boxing out, cutting off and screening opponents must be eliminated. Coaches need to realize that rough play will not be tolerated and officials must rule on all infractions when they occur.

10-7-1 Number 5 is blocking her opponent when she illegally contacts her with her arms in an effort to obstruct movement. A player may not impede the progress of an opponent by extending an arm, shoulder, hip, or knee, or by bending the body into an abnormal position.

10-7-1 Rough play and contact by players attempting to secure a loose ball is a foul. Such contact that negates an opponent's advantageous position is not incidental contact and should be penalized.

10-7-6 Number 32 drives for the basket and takes off for a jump shot. In the two-part PlayPic sequence, number 20 moves forward and under the airborne shooter. The airborne shooter is in the act of shooting until he returns to the floor. When No. 20 moves into the path of an airborne shooter, it results in a foul against a player in the act of shooting. If the try is successful, one free throw is awarded. If the try is unsuccessful, two free throws are awarded.

10-7-6 Number 32 leaps and attempts a jump shot. While No. 32 is airborne, No. 3 takes a position on the court to rebound. Number 32 returns to the court, and his momentum carries him into the back of No. 3 who had obtained a legal position. The foul in (3) is on No. 32. If the try is successful, the goal counts.

10-7-8; 4-40-6 In (1), both players are moving in the same direction and in the same path. In (2), A4 stops and B5 runs into the back of him. This is a foul on B5. In that situation, the player behind is responsible for contact regardless of how abruptly the dribbler stops.

10-7-9 If No. 1 continues her course, she will commit a player-control charging foul. Because No. 1 has the ball, time and distance are of no consequence as No. 3 has obtained legal position by having both feet on the court and facing No. 1.

10-7-9 Defensive player No. 5 may move into the path of a dribbler at any time, provided she is able to obtain a legal position. To initially obtain this position, she must be facing the dribbler with both feet on the floor. Subsequently, she may turn, crouch or retreat in order to avoid injury if she is charged by the dribbler. Number 5 has obtained a legal position. If she maintains her legal position, the dribbler is responsible for any contact.

10-7-12 The following acts constitute a foul when committed against a ball handler/dribbler, post player: two hands on, extended arm bar on, keeping a hand on and contacting more than once.

10-7-12 A player becomes a ball handler/dribbler when he/she receives the ball. This would include a player in a post position.

Start Clock

Stop Clock

Stop Clock for
Held Ball

Stop Clock for Foul

Stop Clock for Foul
(Optional 'Bird Dog')

Directional Signal

Free Throw, Designated Spot or Other Violations

Move Along the Endline

Visible Count

Beckoning Substitutes

60-Second Time-out

30-Second Time-out

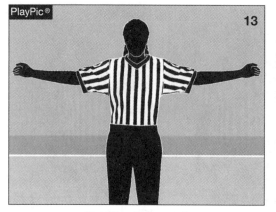

Not Closely Guarded

Tipped Ball

No Score

Goal Counts

Point(s) Scored:
Use 1, 2 or 3 fingers after Signal 16

3-Point Attempt Score
3-Point Attempt Made

Bonus Free Throw

Signal Free Throw
Attempts

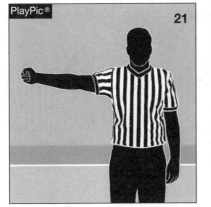

Delayed Lane Violation

Traveling Violation

Illegal Dribble

Palming/Carrying
Violation

Over and Back

3-Second Violation

5-Second Violation

10-Second Violation

Excessively Swinging
Arm(s)/Elbow(s)

Kicking

Illegal Use of Hands

Hand Check

Holding

Blocking

Pushing/Charging

Player-Control Foul

Team-Control Foul

Intentional Foul

Double Foul

Technical Foul

NFHS PUBLICATIONS
Prices effective April 1, 2019 — March 31, 2020

RULES PUBLICATIONS

Baseball Rules Book...$10.00	Ice Hockey Rules Book $10.00
Baseball Case Book..$10.00	Boys Lacrosse Rules Book............................$10.00
Baseball Umpires Manual (2019 & 2020) $10.00	Girls Lacrosse Rules Book $10.00
Baseball Simplified & Illustrated Rules $10.00	Soccer Rules Book..$10.00
Baseball Rules by Topic $10.00	Softball Rules Book...$10.00
Basketball Rules Book....................................$10.00	Softball Case Book..$10.00
Basketball Case Book.....................................$10.00	Softball Umpires Manual (2020 & 2021) $10.00
Basketball Simplified & Illustrated Rules $10.00	Softball Simplified & Illustrated Rules $10.00
Basketball Officials Manual (2019-21) $10.00	Softball Rules by Topic $10.00
Basketball Handbook (2018-20)....................$10.00	Spirit Rules Book $10.00
Basketball Rules by Topic $10.00	Swimming & Diving Rules Book $10.00
Field Hockey Rules Book...............................$10.00	Track & Field Rules Book...............................$10.00
Football Rules Book $10.00	Track & Field Case Book $10.00
Football Case Book...$10.00	Track & Field Manual (2019 & 2020) $10.00
Football Simplified & Illustrated Rules $10.00	Volleyball Rules Book......................................$10.00
Football Handbook (2019 & 2020)................$10.00	Volleyball Case Book & Manual.....................$10.00
Football Game Officials Manual	Volleyball Simplified & Illustrated Rules $10.00
(2018 & 2019) $10.00	Water Polo Rules Book (2018-20) $10.00
Football Rules by Topic..................................$10.00	Wrestling Rules Book......................................$10.00
Girls Gymnastics Rules Book & Manual	Wrestling Case Book & Manual.....................$10.00
(2018-20)...$10.00	

MISCELLANEOUS ITEMS

NFHS Statisticians' Manual $8.00
Scorebooks: Baseball-Softball, Basketball, Swimming & Diving, Cross Country, Soccer,
   Track & Field, Volleyball, Wrestling and Field Hockey $12.00
Diving Scoresheets (pad of 100).. $8.00
Volleyball Team Rosters & Lineup Sheets (pads of 100) $8.00
Libero Tracking Sheet (pads of 50)... $8.00
Baseball/Softball Lineup Sheets – 3-Part NCR (sets/100)... $10.00
Wrestling Tournament Match Cards (sets/100) $7.25
Competitors Numbers (Track and Gymnastics – Waterproof, nontearable, black numbers and
   six colors of backgrounds numbers are 1-1000 sold in sets of 100 .... $15.00/set

MISCELLANEOUS SPORTS ITEMS

Court and Field Diagram Guide $25.00	Sportsmanship. It's Up to You Toolkit $19.95
NFHS Handbook (2018-19)..........................$12.00	High School Activities – A Community
Let's Make It Official $5.00	Investment in America $39.95

ORDERING

Individuals ordering NFHS publications and other products and materials
are requested to order online at **www.nfhs.com**.

National Federation of State High School Associations

2019-20
NFHS RULES BOOKS

Published in 17 sports by the National Federation of State High School Associations, rules books contain the official rules for high school athletic competition. These books are designed to explain all aspects of the game or contest. They are good for participants as well as coaches and contest officials.

The NFHS also publishes case books, manuals, handbooks and illustrated books in several sports to help in further explaining the rules.

Customer Service Department

PO Box 361246, Indianapolis, IN 46236-5324

1-800-776-3462

or order online at **www.nfhs.com**